YOU CAN WRITE A NOVEL

SECOND EDITION

JAMES V. SMITH, JR.

WRITER'S
BOOKS

WritersD
Cincinn

For more resources for writers, visit www.writersdigest.com/books.

To receive a free weekly e-mail newsletter delivering tips and updates about writing and about Writer's Digest products, register directly at http://newsletters.fwpublications.com.

14 13 12 11 10 5 4 3 2 1

Distributed in Canada by Fraser Direct, 100 Armstrong Avenue, Georgetown, Ontario, Canada L7G 5S4, Tel: (905) 877-4411. Distributed in the U.K. and Europe by F+W Media International, Brunel House, Newton Abbot, Devon, TQ12 4PU, England, Tel: (+44) 1626-323200, Fax: (+44) 1626-323319, E-mail: postmaster@davidandcharles. co.uk. Distributed in Australia by Capricorn Link, P.O. Box 704, Windsor, NSW 2756 Australia, Tel: (02) 4577-3555.

Library of Congress Cataloging-in-Publication Data

Smith, James V., 1946-

You can write a novel / by James V. Smith, Jr. -- 2nd ed.

p. cm.

Includes index.

ISBN 978-1-58297-961-8 (pbk. : alk. paper)

1. Fiction--Authorship. 2. Creative writing. I. Title.

PN3365.S64 2010

808.3--dc22

2010029812

Edited by Melissa Hill
Designed by Claudean Wheeler
Cover photograph by joingate/iStockphoto
Production coordinated by Debbie Thomas

DEDICATION

For Dylan, son of my son, Shaun.

ACKNOWLEDGMENTS

Thanks to my agent, Peter Rubie of the Fine Print Literary Agency, who always makes time to visit and encourage.

Thanks to the great professionals at Writer's Digest: editor Melissa Hill, whose enthusiasm kept me fired up and Kim Catanzarite, whose copyediting and tough questions kept me from some boneheaded errors.

Thanks to reader reviewers, who pointed out my flaws in the first edition of this book and the others. You were on my mind in writing this revision. I invite your continued comments at www.workfromparadise.com.

Above all, thanks to my wife, Sue, who let me dodge a lot of household chores on the excuse I had to get this revision done.

And now, I must go. The shrubs grow fast and well past last year's trimming. And I see the weeds—not to mention the lame excuses—have all gone to seed. And, after those chores are done, I have my own novels to write.

TABLE OF CONTENTS

STEP 1: Identify the One-Word Key to Every Best-Seller 1

- Discover the one-word key to your coming writing success. • Adopt a single, unified, game-changing YCWAN concept that will reinvent your writing with its sixteen elements for grabbing readers, dragging them into your novel, and compelling them to talk about it. • Learn to recognize sixteen sins that diminish the sixteen elements of the YCWAN system.

STEP 2: Sketch the First Draft of Your Novel in Only Two Incidents 15

- Learn why you should write Incidents instead of scenes. • And, incidentally, learn what an Incident is and what the two most important Incidents are in your novel. • Structure your story using the YCWAN A to Z method. • Write at least a sketch of your two most important Incidents.

STEP 3: Test Your Novel for Salability 22

- Examine the sixteen elements of participation at work. • Test your novel against the essential elements of a salable novel. • Amp up the essential elements of your novel. • Write a brief Nugget Statement that will focus your efforts in writing and selling your novel.

STEP 4: Invent Key Details to Enrich Your Rough Draft and Smooth the Way for the Rest of Your Novel 43

- Refine a working title. • Add digital cast of characters. • Select names for your characters. • Adopt a point of view.

STEP 5: Get Down to Some Serious Writing 63

- Use the Incident checklist as the basis for writing your plot or story structure. • Rewrite your first draft Incidents using the YCWAN system, especially the ACIIDSS Test. • Evaluate the Opener of a best-seller. • Avoid mistakes of amateurs.

STEP 6: Evaluate Your Opener Incident for Reading Ease and Reader Participation 99

- Edit your Opener Incident using numeric goals as a guide. • Inject precision into your novel by choosing the right words. • Take the first steps to reinvent your writing style. • Scan your Opener for greater reading ease and participation. • Wrie more compact Incidents, starting with your very next one.

STEP 7: Create the Rest of Your Main Story Line as a Series of Headlines 112

- Create the rest of your central story line—structuring the easy way. • Write your Point of No Return Incident. • Develop the Closer Incident further. • Apply the simplest of structures to Incidents, Tragedy Versus Triumph.

STEP 8: Revise Your Novel to Best-Seller Standards 127

- Clean up the mechanics of your novel. • Apply some advanced revision techniques. • Create tie backs and transitions. • Add texture to your story. • Set your words to music.

STEP 9: Market Your Novel by Creating an Irresistible Package That Engages Editors and Agents 146

- Get real about what might happen when you submit your novel. • Identify the selling points of your story. • Analyze the marketplace. • Prepare your pitch. • Prepare your package.

STEP 10: Polish Your Novel to Best-Seller Standards While Your Sales Package Is Out There Pitching for You 157

- Evaluate the pace of every Incident in your novel. • Revise to adjust the pace within each Incident that needs it. • Evaluate the pace of your novel as a whole and graph its intensity level from beginning to end. • Revise as necessary to reset intensity and pace.

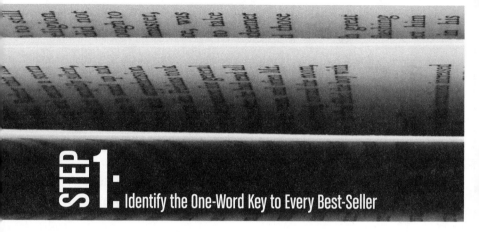

STEP 1: Identify the One-Word Key to Every Best-Seller

Reinvent your writing using one or more of the sixteen elements that make up a dramatic, new breakout concept that drives every best-seller ever written.

Here's what you're going to do in chapter 1.

- Discover the one-word key to your coming writing success.
- Adopt a single, unified, game-changing YCWAN concept that will reinvent your writing with its sixteen elements for grabbing readers, dragging them into your novel, and compelling them to talk about it.
- Learn to recognize sixteen sins that diminish the sixteen elements of the YCWAN system.

YOU *CAN* WRITE A NOVEL

You can, just as our title suggests. And easier than ever before, because this book offers new tools to get the job done, as well as a great process for doing it.

My four previous writing how-to books are toolboxes for writers. Like any toolbox, they contain tools that are common to each. For instance, I put writing rules (hammers) and character cards (tape measures) in each. From book to book, each collection of tools varies. I tossed out an old wrench and added a new file to the toolbox as I went along. And with each new book, I also added a fresh discovery. In this book that's the Reading Ease Ideal (laser tape measure). Such tools have helped writers like you complete and sell their novels. And they've helped me, too, in my own writing, which entails both a job as magazine editor, novelist, and writer of nonfiction.

The reader reviews on Amazon and other sites helped me refine this system. Writers said that my books helped them finish and even sell theirs—one woman who'd sold a novel said: "It could happen to you, too."

Still. All those great tools were in four separate toolboxes.

No more. At last, this revision pulls all the best material from each of my books into a single title. I've tossed a lot of old stuff. No more rules. Instead of hammers, I've gone to cordless power nail guns, so to speak. Plus. I've added a ton of new material that makes writing make better sense to me. Tools you haven't seen before because I've only just invented and revealed them.

Best of all, I've woven all of my ideas into a single unified system that will help you reinvent the way you write. For example, I've placed the Reading Ease Ideal (REI) in the most logical place in this new system with the aim to renew your writing, lift your spirits, and inspire you to write your novel to *The End*. The logic in the book is a road map.

Why, this system makes so much sense, it even makes sense to me. I tend to be lazy, so I've made it easy. So my road map is the shortest possible route between *Once upon a time* and *They all lived happily ever after*.

Which is still just half the task, isn't it? Because you want to do more than *write* your novel. You want to *sell* it.

I have great news for you. The system in this book will help you finish a product that's ready to roll out to agents and editors. Yes …

YOU *CAN* SELL A NOVEL

This goes for you, even if you already are a published novelist. You want to get to the next level, right? A second novel? A move from writing category fiction to a mainstream novel, a truly Great American Novel, well-reviewed, well-respected, and destined for the classics? Or it could be moving up from a midlist spot in the house catalog to the ten-city signing tour status. Or maybe …

Just maybe it's a matter of writing to a new, higher personal standard. Maybe you're a good writer, already, but you know you can do better. If only you knew how. I get it. More than tours and reviews, I want to write better, just as you do. And, yes, I admit it, I want to sell better, too.

Again, I have good news. This book is your next rung up the skill ladder. It's working for me. I'm lucky. My job as editor, writer, photographer, website administrator, and window washer at *Rural Montana*, the largest circulation publication in Montana, demands that I write every day. It's my proving grounds for writing ideas. And it's my sounding board, literally. My readers sound off. *Rural Montana* goes to 120,000 households and a readership of nearly twice that, our surveys say. People report what they like and what they don't. That feedback helps me test my system and adjust. Month to month.

So these tools are field tested. I invented many of them in just the past year or so. Some I tweak every month. In other words, you're getting cutting-edge writing technology here. Some of these tools will seem experimental, even wild. All of them are grounded in reality. I'll be using all of them to write the next novel I submit to my agent.

Am I asking you to dream? Well, yes, I suppose. But more than that, I prefer to think of it as a journey—one which starts with that road map. This book.

Our road map is a ten-step process. Check out the contents page of this book. Those chapter headings are the ten steps you'll take to writing your novel.

Now, let's get going.

WHAT'S THAT ONE-WORD KEY TO BEST-SELLING FICTION?

It begins with readers, so let's first talk about them. The key to best-selling fiction is in this quote.

> "'Why do people enjoy fiction?' (This) is identical to the question 'Why do people enjoy life?' When we are absorbed in a book or a movie, we get to see breathtaking landscapes, hobnob with important people, fall in love with ravishing men and women, protect loved ones, attain impossible goals, and defeat wicked enemies. Not a bad deal for seven dollars and fifty cents!"
>
> —STEVEN PINKER, *How the Mind Works*

Did you pick up on it? Do you know the word you're looking for? No? Here, let me help you find it.

The Key to Every Best-Seller Ever Written

When I tell you to, put down this book and e-rocket through the Internet to the most useful database ever known to writers. Try either www.amazon.com or www.barnesandnoble.com. Select a best-seller in fiction, classic or current.

Anything with a history of a hundred or more reader reviews. Try a best-seller in nonfiction as well.

Go to the reader reviews of the best-seller you select. Try the newest reviews first, for starters. That way you won't be reading a shill review by the author's Granny Fanny. Look at one-star reviews as well as five-star reviews. The answer is in both types.

Your mission? To pick out the one-word quality that is the key to every best-seller that ever was or ever will be. Find it or guess at it from what you read in the reviews.

Ready? Put down this book and come back later to check your answer against mine. Don't cheat. This mission is your first little step in getting to the next level in your writing. If you skip this step, you will skip an important lesson. I can't teach the lesson unless you're willing to learn it.

Go.

Back already?

Did you learn the answer to the question?

What One Word Describes What Readers Find To Love In Every Best-Seller?

Not to out-Socrates Socrates, but let's dig deeper; answer another question. Did you ever *write* a review on Amazon? If you did, I'll bet it's for one of three reasons.

One, you're working at earning a top ranking among the reader reviewers. Which earns you a T-shirt or a coffee cup with your name on it. Which is just truly wonderful, but beside my teaching point. So, let's talk about the other two reviewer types.

Two, you love a book and found it useful.

Three, you hate a book.

The first reviewer type comes at the task from the head. It's a purely intellectual thing, a chance to show off a lit degree, a big bookshelf, or a big brain.

But, reader reviewers who either love a book or hate a book fly at it on wings of the heart. One guy loves the author's best-seller from last year. So last year's review was a lovefest. This year's best-seller is a cheat, and our guy is mad as hell, and he isn't going to take one of that author's books home anymore. He writes a toxic review.

On the other hand, a best-selling novelist brings a woman to tears, and she feels compelled to say so. She writes a sobbing thank-you to the writer who touched her soul.

Each of those actions is a fairly strong hint about my one-word key to reinventing your writing.

So, what did you come up with in picking the one-word quality that is the key to a best seller? Was it one of these words or phrases?

1. Emotion?
2. Interest?
3. Powerful characters?
4. Fast-paced page-turner? (Versus *boring*, which does appear often in reader reviews)
5. Engaging plot?
6. Inability to sleep?
7. Fun?
8. Intrigue?
9. Powerful writing?
10. Ability to make you laugh, cry, sweat, retch?

Never mind that many of these are phrases instead of single words. I find them to be all good answers. And part of the right answer. Just not the right answer in full. Try putting them together. Take those ten qualities, plus any of your own, and collect them into a single one-word quality that embraces every one of the millions of readers who make best-sellers sell.

Hint: You won't find your answers in the books themselves. It's not about writing alone. Or authors. Or categories.

The answer is in the readers. Literally. Inside their minds and hearts and souls. The readers who report their emotions in reviews on Amazon and other sites are telling you what they love—or hate—about what they find in their reading. They are literally helping you create your own road map to writing successful fiction.

BOTTOM LINE: HERE IS THE ONE-WORD KEY TO ALL BEST-SELLING WRITING

Factual or fictional. Past, present, or future, it's not what the writer puts into a novel as much as what the reader gets out of it. Namely, a feeling of …

PARTICIPATION

In fact, the writing of any kind that people read first and most voraciously, whether an office memo, an advertisement, a piece of fiction, or a nonfiction book is writing that matters to them personally. They have to care about something in the writing.

Quick example. A memo from *The Boss*.

TO: All Employees

SUBJECT: You park in my spot again and you're *FIRED!!*

Signed: The Boss

Now about that caring. If you ride the bus, you don't care about the memo. You don't park in any spot, so literally you have no reason to care unless the guilty party is either your friend or your enemy.

Or in the other case … if you've been parking in front of The BOSS-Only sign, you care enough to find a new spot. You care a lot. You respond to the writing. You run right out and move your car.

In books, the writing that takes the personal interest to the next level of participation is the writing that is read most often, bought most often, and talked about most often, leading to our unified concept of the best-seller. Drum roll, please, for … **Participation.**

The stories that engage readers most sell best.

The greater the participation, the better the seller.

Wait, you say. *What about the writing and the characters? Doesn't the writing matter? Aren't the characters key?*

If you're like me, you've spent years writing under the weight of these illusions, so you'd better take a seat. Brace yourself.

About the writing? Frankly, nice as nice writing is, and much as we like it when we read it, good writing simply is not the decisive factor in making a book a best-seller. Sorry. Writing doesn't matter as much as we'd like to the business of selling millions of books. Lots of beautifully written books fail to become best-sellers. And lots of drivel makes it to the top of best-seller lists. In your heart you know this, and I feel your pain.

Characters? Characters matter. A lot. But you can get by without great ones. Much as we liked the great ones in the very best novels we've read.

Think about it. You've read writing that reeks in many a best-seller. One of the many knocks on Dan Brown's *The Da Vinci Code*, a huge best-seller, is that it was not all that well written. And, if you go check the reader reviews of his latest best-seller, *The Lost Symbol*, even many of his adoring *TDVC* fans aren't fond of the newer book. (*We should have his paydays, though, eh?*) They tell you flat out the characters are thin and lifeless as an expired credit card and the writing is boring, dull, overwrought, and worse. And yet those books sold millions.

How? I say *participation*. Participation is larger, much larger than either writing or characters. Or category.

Am I saying that you don't have to be a good writer to sell a novel? In fact, yes. Writing well can help. And I will do all I can to pump up your writing and my own, but we can sell our novels even if we don't have the writing talent of a literary giant. To prove it, I offer this …

REAL-LIFE CASE STUDY IN HORRIBLE

I once went looking for a job at a publishing house. Part of my prehire test was to look at a sample book proposal and respond to the author, give him some advice on how to work over his story idea, and decide whether to accept it at the house. In turn, the hiring team would evaluate my evaluation.

Right away I knew it was a fake proposal worked out by the editors at the house. They must have had a great time at the meeting to devise the test. I pictured them pounding on the table, laughing out loud, trying to catch their breath in the middle of group hysteria, falling out of their chairs, literally rolling on the floor laughing, *LOL* and *ROFL*, as they say in texting shorthand.

I figured they threw in parts of every bad manuscript ever submitted by author wannabes, as well as made-up stuff.

The writing stunk. The logic was bizarre. And the idea was goofy. Every tenth word was misspelled. The editors must have used a book of clichés to build their test by stringing them together. "Oh, wait," one of them must have said. "Let's throw in some stick-men drawings. Look, I'm doing one left-handed."

It was that bad. I did my best, kept a fake straight face, tried to inspire the fake author, and sent the fake offering back with a fake polite rejection. Then I had a laugh myself, writing in my fake rejection, "If you would like to consider my edits and resubmit, by all means contact me again." I mean, I can write some fiction, too, people.

Above all, I knew the sample was just a test. I had to give the hiring staff an answer. I couldn't expect to get hired at a house by sending them a standard rejection form, could I?

I got the interview. Got a job offer. Asked, "Just out of curiosity, what about that fake manuscript I graded?"

"That wasn't a fake."

In fact, it became one of their best-sellers. Granted, it was a small house that specialized in just the kind of goofy idea that the author had sent in. They were willing to put in a lot of editorial work and even hire a book doctor on behalf of the author.

Crazy, huh?

What's not so crazy is this: You don't have to be a literary giant to write a best-seller, let alone sell one.

Bottom line: Have faith, people. You really can do this. You should write as well as you can. Of course you should. But you don't need to be an Anne Tyler or Alice Sebold or Cormac McCarthy or Stephen King, good writers all and best-selling authors besides.

All you need do is ...

MODEL THE WRITING SECRETS OF THOSE VERY BEST-SELLERS

Think. Ever notice that all kinds of writing from all kinds of authors can lead to best-selling fiction?

In an earlier book for Writer's Digest, I did a semi-scientific study of best-selling authors to see what they had in common. I could not explain why Danielle Steel and Stephen King were best-sellers alongside Pulitzer Prize-winning novelists Larry McMurtry and Wallace Stegner. We do know they all have instincts, style, and mechanics that yield very high reader participation.

Can you use their devices? To quote from the film, *Fargo: You betcha.* This book will show you how you can model their work and boost your chances of getting agents, editors, and many, many readers to fall in love with your book.

I know. Accepting this *not-great-writing-can-sell* thing is a thick swallow, so let me pitch at you from another angle. George Orwell, in an essay titled, "Good Bad Books," writes:

> "(this is) the kind of book that has no literary pretensions but which remains readable when more serious productions have perished."

Oh, and here's Orwell in a 1936 review of *Walls Have Mouths*:

> "This is a remarkable book. It is formless and badly written, but packed full of the kind of details that matter."

Think. Read it again. Think again. What kind of terrific review might Orwell have given this book, had the writer showed solid form and singing prose besides details that matter? The same goes for you. You can use form, writing, and details that matter to engage readers. To make them participate in your story might matter more than writing. Paraphrasing from an old comedy sketch: Remember this point and don't ever forget it:

THE POWER OF PARTICIPATION

Participation alone can do more for selling your novel than writing or characters or plot or style or any other quality or element that you've been reading and learning about your (and my) whole, misguided writership life.

That's why, from now on, I'll make participation the central focus of this revision of YCWAN.

An aside: For those of you firing up the keyboard to flame me for saying that good writing doesn't matter, use your emotion in your writing and not as a weapon of fire against me. I didn't say writing doesn't matter. Rather, I'm saying other things can matter even more. Again, borrowing from *Saturday Night Live*: *Simmah down now.*

Stick with me, and I'll nail down this concept for you. Think about all the great books that swept you away. Somehow, the writer gave you a part to play, even if only as a close observer of the story. You laugh at the people in the book. Or maybe you laugh with them. When they are in danger, you sweat it. When they suffer setbacks, you agonize.

You never forget the great novels, that is, the ones that made you participate in this story. Or maybe it was, after all, the terrific writing that made you sigh or cry, but—it wasn't just the writing. Rather that it made you sigh or cry. These books touched you, heart and soul.

Again. And again …

You Can Sell Even If You Don't Write Well

Flash back to Orwell and think about all the not-great books, even poorly written books, that have shallow characters that still became best-sellers. Take

The Da Vinci Code. Some kind of magic was at work among millions of readers. I admit, I did not like the book. To borrow from a *Seinfeld* episode: It wasn't that I'm Catholic that offended me about *The Da Vinci Code*; it was that, like you, I like to think of myself as a writer. *The Da Vinci Code* didn't cut it for me. Still, I had to find out why it worked for so many other people. I forced myself to read it to the end. At times, parts of that story did interest me. Turns out, I love puzzles. Anagrams. I got involved trying to work those out before the hero did. Whereas the plot contrivances bugged me, the puzzles were kind of fun.

As I developed my insight that participation is the key to best-selling status, something came on in my head like the blue light special at Kmart. *The Da Vinci Code is participation in P-A-S-S-E-D*. Get it? It's all about readers playing a part, either in Dan Brown's anagrams or mine. Meaning *The Da Vinci Code is participation in S-P-A-D-E-S*.

Remember the show, *Who Wants to Be a Millionaire?* that later became a vehicle to carry the stories in *Slumdog Millionaire?* Remember how it first hit America like a tidal wave? Do you know why it was such a rage?

It's the $100 question, of course. Literally.

Remember how it went? *Okay, Billy Bob, for $100: Purple is a) White, b) A shade of black, c) A color all its own, or d) The color of a novel.*

Okay, that would probably be a $1,000 question because it has two tricks in it instead of just the one. But my point is this—Merv Griffin invented this game show so that any idiot could play a round or two at home in the early stages. It became a contest later, as viewers try to outguess the people who advance to more difficult levels. Why not take a stab at the answer when you don't have anything to lose? Or shout at the TV set, "*You goofball. Take the money and run.*" Do you see it now? Do you see the participation?

Game shows don't work just because people like to see prizes and pretty women turning letters. Game shows work because viewers can play along. Which is to say *participate*.

That very form of playing along is how Dan Brown made his novels a success, too. And I don't mean it's a close call, either. It's the exact dynamic. He was so inventive, so creative, so brilliant in making up puzzles and plot twists and weaving fact and myth into a tale in which millions played along. So much so that good writing and rich characters did not matter to them.

Great theory, you say. *But ...*

HOW DO WE GET THERE FROM HERE?

How, indeed. For the rest of this book, the *how* is my job. Your job is to learn the process. I'll teach you dozens of ways to put this concept to work in your own story. You apply them every chance you get. And, yes, you should write as well as you can, too.

I'll start by naming my sixteen elements of participation. And I'll add just one writerly sin against each element, comments you can find in a brief scan of Amazon reader reviews. We'll further define, refine, develop, and start using the elements and avoiding the sins in each chapter that follows.

The Sixteen Elements of Participation

1. **Precision**—absolute clarity in words and ideas. Just as it's a sin to kill a mockingbird, it's a sin to let readers say your words and ideas were: *vague and confusing.*

2. **Action**—at all times. If you can't move a mountain, at least move an arm or even an eyebrow. Sin: *The story dragged.*

3. **Relevance**—make your writing matter to readers. Sin: *Who cares?*

4. **Tales**—towering and tiny tales, lots of them and all within the context of the main story. The sin in three words: *Blah, blah, blah.*

5. **Imagery**—more than description, the vivid pictures in readers' minds. Sin: *I skipped huge sections of description; no need to take note of every hair and freckle of every waiter who brings a glass of water.*

6. **Conflict**—in all things great and small. Sin: *Boring. I put this book down and couldn't make myself pick it up again.*

7. **Irony**—a sense of humor as well as larger thematic irony. Sin: *The arrogant writer and catty heroine take themselves too seriously.*

8. **Pacing**—a feeling that a story moves, varying from slow to fast at the proper times. Sin: *Narcolepsy. I picked up this book when I wanted to get to sleep fast.*

9. **Aspiration**—or Angels, as in an appeal to the better angels of our nature. Sin: *Everybody in the story is a creep with no redeeming qualities. For Pete's sake, I hated everybody, even the hero.*

10. **Tone**—a lyrical or rhythmic feel in the writing—you see, I do think strong writing is an element of participation, but just one of the sixteen. Sin: *No poetry; full of cliches.*

11. **Ideal**—the Reading Ease Ideal, a tool for editing and revision to model best-selling writing. (We'll talk more about this in chapter six.) Sin: *Writing you'd find in a term paper or dissertation.*

12. **Only two thousand words**—a suggestion only to change the subject as often as every two thousand words to keep the interest of readers who are growing up as members of the Twitter-Facebook-texting-random-browsing generation. Sin: *I thought it was plagiarism to copy long passages from an encyclopedia.*

13. **Novelty**—the sense that this is a new story with something new on every other page. Sin: *Haven't I read this novel before?*

14. **Surprise**—that frequent feeling of *Oh! Wow!* the best-sellers always have. Sin: *Predictable. I had the mystery figured out two hundred pages before the hero.*

15. **Questions**—as simple as it sounds, simply asking questions of readers to get them to play along. Sin: *I never quite got into the story.*

16. **Dialogue**—and I do mean *great* dialogue between characters and between characters and readers. Sin: *I got tired of the heroine's sermons.*

There you go. The sixteen elements of participation and sixteen comments you never want to hear about your own novel. Several new concepts. The basis for a complete YCWAN system, one that will help you avoid the sins.

Test These Elements Again

For your own sake, go back to Amazon and take a look at those reader reviews a second time. This participation concept is crucial. You need to see the participation working in a best-seller. Start with a best-seller that has lots of negative reviews, something that averages two to three stars. I'll bet you find mention of many more than one of the sins against the elements of participation listed above.

Then choose a novel that swept you away. One you want to model in its success, using this book as your guide. There you'll find the same elements as virtues. *I couldn't put this novel down.* Or, *I lost sleep.* Or, *This author was writing her own love letter to me.* Like that.

Did you see what I'm talking about? When a reader reports that she loves a novel, she often mentions how she played a part in it. She cried with the heroine. She trembled at the villain. She found that her life was in sync with the hero's. She lost sleep. She let the dishes pile up in the sink. She wrote: "*I could hardly wait to get home from work and neglect my kids.*"

When a reader reports that he hates the novel, you can see that it is because it gave him no part to play. It was boring to read about other people playing, leaving him no way to connect. Not only did he not play a part in the story in any way, not even as a voyeur, but he also felt the author cheated him out of his twenty bucks. You can almost hear him saying, "*I was gypped.*" In fact, reviewers say that quite often.

In either case, love or hate, it's personal.

If the reader spends $10 or $20, or even as little as $7.50, as Pinker suggests in his quote earlier in this chapter, he may not say so in so many words, but he expects that you will leave open the door to his playing a part in your novel.

If a reader invests hours upon hours in reading your novel, losing sleep and even taking a sick day, it's because she feels some form of participation. She responds to you reaching out and touching her heartstrings, engaging her emotions, allowing her to participate in the story. Give her somebody to love in your book. Give her somebody to hate. Give her night sweats. For a long time after she finishes reading, trouble her. Or uplift her. Either way, let her play a part in the life of your story.

Participation: Give readers a part to play in your story. Move them to action. Force them to play along with your characters.

You do this, and they will pay you back. Not just with a few dollars they spend on your book, but with word-of-mouth marketing. The most powerful reward any novelist can hope for: *The Buzz.*

There you go. It's all about participation.

Caution: It won't be easy for you to buy in to some of these more edgy tips. You'll have to write outside the lines, break some habits, some of them good. You're going to have to cut against the grain of your brain. Read on and I'll show you what I mean.

GET OUT OF YOUR COMFORT ZONE

Try this exercise in breaking an old habit. Fold your arms across your chest. Notice which of your forearms is on top. If you're like most people, it will be your right arm. When I say, *Go*, put down this book and refold your arms the opposite way. If you're right was on top, fold so that your left is on top. And vice versa.

Go.

Not so easy to do, is it? Then, when you do finally get it done, it just doesn't feel right. Right?

I'll be suggesting some things in this book that will make your brain feel as awkward as your arms did a moment ago. Don't worry. Refolding your brain won't hurt you anymore than refolding your arms did. In fact, it's going to open your mind's eyes to a whole new way of writing and storytelling.

People, we are going to reinvent your writing.

Saddle up, boys and girls. Let's get to work on it.

Write the two most important Incidents in your story's structure so you have something to build from—and build toward—as you write future Incidents.

Here's what you're going to do in chapter 2.

- Learn why you should write Incidents instead of scenes.
- And, incidentally, learn what an Incident is and what the two most important Incidents are in your novel.
- Structure your story using the YCWAN *A to Z* method.
- Write at least a sketch of your two most important Incidents.

START WRITING

I mean it. Start writing. Get a pair of sketches down in a file or on paper. No rules. No examples. No advice. Just write.

In the first edition of this book, I suggested that you prepare in detail before you start writing. In this revised book, I'm taking a simpler approach. Most writers are eager to begin writing. So I say, *Get to it.* I think it's more fun and more useful if you can empty your brain of ideas for your novel first. Then we have two things to work with: First, the blank slate of your brain after you've put your thoughts down on paper or into a digital file; second some rough writing which we will evaluate, enlarge, revise, shape, and make sing. That, in fact, is the very plan of this book.

WRITE INCIDENTS, NOT SCENES

Think of your novel in terms of *Incidents*. By which I also mean, forget the term *scenes*. Start thinking in terms of *Incidents*.

I rely on Mark Twain for the insight:

> Incidents are better, any time, than dry history.

This is one of those arm-folding tricks I'm playing on your brain, so just go along with me. *Scene* is a sterile term about a writing device. In contrast, an *Incident* is something that happens. *Incident* implies drama, things going wrong, conflict, people in trouble. It's a word right out of a police report. Trauma, conflict, action, Incident. That's where we want to be. You're a writer who is learning to tell stories Incident by Incident, with conflict and action built right into the term.

You might as well start thinking Incidents, capital *I*, because I'm not going to use the word, *scene*, anymore in this book, except to refer to it as history.

The top three critical, or Master, Incidents in your novel:

1. **The opening Incident.** Call it your big fat Greek **Opener**, if it helps you remember.

2. **The Point-of-No-Return Incident, PoNRI for short.** We won't deal with the PoNRI now, except for a couple mentions. Which leaves …

3. **The climactic Incident, or climax.** Call it your All-American Kick-Butt **Closer**. For my purposes, it includes the resolution of the story. But let's not complicate things for now.

I used to tell writers to think of a novel's basic structure in only ten scenes. Not anymore. It was Thoreau who advised, "Simplify, simplify."

So let's cut those ten scenes down to size. Think of your novel's timeline as Incidents in the alphabet, with the three letters, *ADZ*, standing out:

A BC D EFGHIJKLMNOPQRSTUVWXY Z

Where A is the Opener to your novel, say, the front bumper of the bus you're trying to pack with readers; D is the Point of No Return Incident, a pivotal point in the story, and fairly far forward in your novel, say, at about the fuzzy stuffed Garfield ornament hanging from your bus's rearview mirror; and Z is the Closer at the tale end, which seals the deal with your reader and leaves tire treads on her mind.

By the way, I'd include the story's resolution as part of the Closer. And, I do mean for the relative size of the three letters above to mean something to you. Size refers to importance. Clearly, the Opener is important for snagging and holding readers, especially agents and editors. I say the Closer is most important of all on the road to best-seller status because, although it's crucial for a reader to feel connected to your story the first moment she picks it up, it's utterly critical how she feels after she turns the last page and sets your novel down. Why? Because you want her to sign on to your sales team, and to talk up your novel to all her friends and fam.

Later we'll discuss the relative size of other letters, too. Many of them will be pivotal points as well.

Also, as we shall see, the PoNRI isn't locked in at D. It can move farther forward, to B or even A and even a novel's first sentence, as it is in *Slumdog Millionaire*. But for now, just get the picture of ADZ. This is your simplest blueprint for a novel.

Now listen to Mark Twain's remarks about episodes, or Incidents A and Z, from his essay, "Fenimore Cooper's Literary Offenses."

> There are nineteen rules governing literary art in the domain of romantic fiction—some say twenty-two. In *Deerslayer* Cooper violated eighteen of them. These eighteen require:
>
> 1. The tale shall accomplish something and arrive somewhere. But the *Deerslayer* tale accomplishes nothing and arrives in the air.
>
> 2. They require that the episodes of the tale shall be necessary parts of the tale, and shall help to develop it. But as the *Deerslayer* tale is not a tale, and accomplishes nothing and arrives nowhere, the episodes have no rightful place in the work, since there was nothing for them to develop.

Nowhere. Think of it as a place you never want your novel to be. That's why I suggest sketching your Closer right from the top. Write a sketch of the Opener and the Closer now—it's even simpler than ADZ—it's as simple as … A to Z.

The YCWAN A to Z Method of Structuring

Yes, write your beginning and ending first, your Opener and Closer. Write as much as you like or as little. Call it a sketch, if that will relax you. With the tools I'm about to give you, you can work with a sample of any size. You just need to know where you will start your story. And where you will end it.

Take it easy on yourself. If you look at writing a novel as one huge project, it can leach the starch right out of your spine. Shel Silverstein answered the question of how to eat a whale in a kid's poem: You eat a whale a bite at a time.

Same with writing a novel. It's not one enormous whale of a project at all. It's simply one bite, one *task*, at a time. If you can identify the two *most* critical of critical Incidents in your story, believe me, everything else will fall into place.

Get both sketches onto a single page of a tablet or a single screen of your text file, if you like. You need only a fist-sized chunk of clay to mold into a sculpture, stroke by stroke, adding pinches of clay as you go. You may later change, or even replace, these Incidents. Doesn't matter. Right now you need a place to start.

If you can do it, sketch your Closer first. More likely you'll already have written a first chapter—closets all over America are filled with first chapters from would-be novelists. Dust it off. Touch it up. Then move on to your Closer.

Still reading? Looking for a different answer? I assure you, I'm serious. Think of this exercise as a rough pencil sketch on the back of an envelope. Later you can turn it into a wonderful landscape you plan to paint in oils. Don't worry about spelling, or form or format. No right answers. No wrong answers. Go on, get to work. Come back when you're finished with your two sketches, and we'll work on them together.

STOP READING HERE. WRITE YOUR FIRST TWO SKETCHES.

Are you finished? Good. Now that you have written these two first major Incidents, even if it's just as sketches, you have, in effect, written a rough first draft of your novel. More important, you have the bookends to your story. If things work out for you the way I want them to, they will contain your story. They are the simplest form of a road map to guide your writing journey. Congratulations.

Don't worry that it's rough. I'm about to give you some tools to juice up both Incidents. But here, up front, I want to teach you to …

AVOID THE JACK TORRANCE SYSTEM OF WRITING

You remember Jack Torrance, don't you? In the Stephen King book and movie, *The Shining*, he sat down to type his novel at page 1, tore a few pages out of the typewriter, crumpled them, and threw them on the floor. Suffered writer's block to the point of madness. Plowed through his writer's block like a Sno-Cat, and settled down to writing like a machine, page after page after page.

If you try to tackle it from page 1, and you're not using a system, you might end up as Jack Torrance did, throwing a lot of paper on the floor, going mad, and writing five hundred or so pages of a single sentence: *All work and no play make Jack a dull boy.*

I will concede that the true writing genius, like Mozart in music, might compose a work of art in his head, then set it down on paper from beginning to end. Fine. If you're the Mozart of words, you don't need this book.

But you don't have to be a rare genius to write a salable novel. All you need is a system that works. So let's get back to work.

The two sketches you've just written take us in a different direction. We'll develop each of them.

After that, we'll build the rest of your story an Incident at a time, weaving the plot from Incident to Incident. Once we get past the three most critical Incidents, I'll cut you loose to write Incidents that interest you the most. Each time you identify an Incident that you must write to make sense of your story, you'll work on that.

That makes writing more fun. But, at any time you need to go back and add details to your Opener or your Closer—or any other Incident—you can feel free to do so. In that way, he will always keep new material tied to your original plan. Proving my point …

The YCWAN System Is Flexible!

You can adopt new and better plot points anytime you wish. If you must change the Closer because you've found a great new sidekick for the hero, just do it.

The YCWAN System Is Efficient!

It …

PREVENTS OVERWRITING. Think about it. If you begin stringing beads, that is, writing the first master Incident, then a minor Incident, then some narrative followed by another minor Incident, then a major Incident before getting to the second master Incident, and so on, you might well reach 80,000 words before you're halfway through your master Incidents. At that point you'll find yourself projecting a novel of 160,000 words or more, an unsalable proposition for a first time novelist—you should shoot for 70,000 to 90,000 words tops.

Where do you go from 160,000 words, though? Write 80,000 more words and cut the finished draft in half? Or cut the first half in two and write the second half in a newly economical style? That's a tough task either way and a lot of wasted time and effort. I say, write only as much as you need to to tell the complete story. No more, no less. This system will help you keep to that standard.

MAINTAINS FOCUS. If you write only two master Incidents on a first draft, you will remain true to the continuity of your story. You will avoid one of the deepest pitfalls of novice writers: going off on tangents. You want tangents? Subplots? Fine. Develop them after you've nailed the A to Z of your novel. Go on to ADZ. Then maybe B. Or even M. Your call. And you'll have the satisfaction of knowing that A will always be at the front of your story and Z will always be the bookend at The End.

SUSTAINS YOUR ENTHUSIASM. Don't drown yourself in writing narrative and minor Incidents to move characters from one situation to another. You'll wish you were already at the next Incident, where the heroine confronts her husband with her discovery of his affair and breaks his jaw in a fistfight. If you find yourself in such a predicament, stop, drop what you're doing, and roll ahead to where you want to be. If the writing is not fun for you, imagine how it's going to feel to the reader. Write the Incident you want to write, your favorite Incident. Then your next favorite. And the next, and so on. Come back later to write the transition.

MINIMIZES WRITING THE STUFF PEOPLE SKIP. It's Elmore Leonard who says, "Don't write the stuff people skip." Indeed. Think about those jokes that go: "So the salesgirl goes to the second farmhouse and … " Doesn't it drive you nuts when the setup of the joke gets repeated at farmhouse after farmhouse? Don't you find yourself mentally windmilling your hands in front of the joke teller's face? Don't you just want to scream, "Get to the punch line"? Good advice. Forget the *blah, blah, blah* of a setup. Write one best punch line (master Incident) after another.

SETS UP TRANSITIONS, TIE BACKS, AND MOTIVATIONS. For example, you write your fifth master Incident and realize that your heroic character has inherited a herd of llamas without you saying how his favorite Peruvian uncle has died (or even that he had an uncle living in the Andes). No problem. Make a note of it and go on to write your sixth favorite master Incident. Worry about creating and burying the uncle later.

If you buy my idea, and if you have your first two Incidents done at least in sketch, we'll move on ... after we deal with that bugaboo ...

WRITER'S BLOCK

I used to pooh-pooh writer's block as a bad case of the lazies. After reading Mark Twain's bio, I realize it can be fear, too. Prolific as Twain was, he stayed away from writing stories that drew on the most painful parts of his life. I get that.

I also think I have the cure. No matter how imposing the fears that want to block you, just write something. Write a poem to the person who caused you pain. List the best and worst of times that apply to your tale. Write a few lines of dialogue. Writing takes on its own life, if you let it. So do.

Don't feel bad about being blocked. But don't let it rule you. Write something. And let's move on, shall we?

STEP 3: Test Your Novel for Salability

See how the elements of participation come into play in best-selling fiction and evaluate your own novel.

Here's what you're going to do in chapter 3.

- Test your story against the sixteen elements of participation.
- Test your novel against the essential elements of a salable novel.
- Amp up the essential elements of your novel.
- Write a brief Nugget Statement that will focus your efforts the rest of the way in writing and selling your novel.

BE GLAD THAT SELLING A NOVEL ISN'T EASY

Here's a little insider insight. Before I ever sold my first novel back in 1980 or so, all I ever heard was, "Fiction is such a hard sell right now." Over the years, the only outlook I've ever heard on fiction from agents that I've worked with (more than half a dozen) are those very words. It's always a hard sell. The editors' take on it is, "We're not buying much fiction now."

Here's something you may *not* have heard before: *I'm glad it's hard.* It keeps out the shade tree writers.

Besides, if writing a novel was as easy as tweeting on Twitter, any fool could do it. And the going rate for a contract would be as valuable as one of those letters asking you to help a Crown Prince get his fortune out of Nigeria by depositing it in your bank—half of which he will share with you, if you will only share your account number first.

Whether writing comes easy or hard to you, a good piece of work will stand out. And what is a good piece of work? A piece of writing that can engage a reader, latching on like Gorilla Glue, peeling off your fingerprints before it lets go. (*Ask me how I know that.*)

Likewise, hard or easy, participation can sell. You boost your chances, if you think about participation from the start. Participation goes into every level of the sale. Not just at the counter in the airport or bookstore. But with the package that you propose to an agent or editor.

Listen again to Mark Twain about James Fenimore Cooper and his *Deerslayer*.

> *Deerslayer* is just simply a literary delirium tremens.
>
> A work of art? It has no invention; it has no order, system, sequence, or results; it has no lifelikeness, no thrill, no stir, no seeming of reality; its characters are confusedly drawn, and by their acts and words they prove that they are not the sort of people the author claims that they are; its humor is pathetic; its pathos is funny; its conversations are—oh! Indescribable; its love scenes odious; its English a crime against the language.
>
> Counting these out, what is left is Art. I think we must all admit that.

For me, the irony is this: On one hand, it's a striking example of many of the problems Cooper might have solved using the ideas that I developed in my concept of participation for selling his novel. On the other hand, art or no, *Deerslayer* was popular in its time. It spent many years on high school literature lists. And it became a popular movie in 1992, staying fairly true to all the defects that Mark Twain pointed out.

Why was it a big seller for all that time? I'd argue that it was the novelty and drama of the way of life on the early frontier, a kind of *Star Wars* of its time. City folks, who knew nothing of the frontier and could not Google to fact-check Cooper's inventions, surely thought they were partaking (participating) in a frontier novel. Hard sell or not, a story can sell even with defects.

Imagine how you can increase your chances if you avoid such defects. You already know the one word that can help you, the key that's name is *participation*.

Now let's talk about how you can use its elements as we move on to develop your first two sketches.

PARTICIPATION PART II – GETTING READERS TO TAKE PART IN YOUR STORY

I've been gnawing at this topic for a long time, trying to get at the core of participation. In in my last how-to, *The Writer's Little Helper*, I provided a list of what readers want. I talked about twenty-five traits in best-selling writing, traits I took from my study of hundreds of reader reviews. Ever since then, I (and maybe you) have been scratching the hair off my head trying to figure out how best to use that list. Finally, I broke the code with my list of sixteen elements of the big picture. Which, in acronym form, I call …**PARTICIPATIONS?"**

I've already introduced the sixteen terms and the sins against them. Now let's look at them again, this time shining our flashlights on their virtues. I'll show some examples from two existing novels. One is *Gone Tomorrow*, a Jack Reacher novel by veteran Lee Child. The other is *Moonlight in Odessa* by Janet Skeslien Charles, a debut novelist. I suggest you read each of them

The Sixteen Elements of PARTICIPATIONS?"

PRECISION. In words and ideas. Be original. Be fresh. Avoid the vague. Choose the concrete. Heed George Orwell in his essay, "Politics and the English Language":

> "A scrupulous writer, in every sentence that he writes, will ask himself these questions: What am I trying to say? What words will express it? Could I put it more shortly? Have I said anything that is avoidably ugly?"

Lee's first words in *Gone Tomorrow*, in the voice of Jack Reacher:

> Suicide bombers are easy to spot.

Two paragraphs later we learn:

> The list is twelve points long if you're looking at a male suspect. Eleven, if you're looking at a woman. The difference is a fresh shave. Male bombers take off their beards. It helps them blend in. Makes them less suspicious. The result is a paler skin on the lower half of the face. No recent exposure to the sun.
> But I wasn't interested in shaves.
> I was working on the eleven-point list.
> I was looking at a woman.

Jack Reacher, the narrator, teaches you something in precise terms and, by the way, adds a nifty surprise. He's not writing from a policy manual. He's setting up action to come. You are into this story. Participating.

The bottom line is that Lee Child never writes in circles, either to obscure plot points or to fake a literary style (although he does sneak a quote from Macbeth into his Opener). Jack Reacher shoots straight. He's easy to follow. You always get the feeling you're learning something from him as you go along for the ride.

ACTION. If stuff happens on every page, in every paragraph, in every sentence of your writing, readers stick with it. They expect action. They read past details that don't matter. Readers want stories to move. Let me tell you how this works, first, in a static scenario. Suppose I write:

> You rent the DVD of *Slumdog Millionaire* and watch it.

Now a second scenario.

> You slap down your five bucks to rent *Slumdog Millionaire*, race home with the DVD, pop the popcorn, drench it in butter, snap the tab on a sweaty cold drink can, poke the *play* button on your DVD, and dry your palms on the sofa fabric every 30 seconds or so for two hours. With your wife glaring at you, until finally she says, "I told you to stop wiping your greasy hands on the couch. Didn't I?"

Do you see how I wrote those two examples? The second one is chock-full of detail. Make stuff happen, and readers participate. (*Er … would you excuse me for a moment? I have to run to the kitchen to pop and butter up some popcorn.*)

I'm not saying you can't write the quick-cut narrative line like the first example. In fact, that might be the best way between two important points. I'm merely showing you how an Incident full of action reads better than dry history.

RELEVANCE. The stuff you write matters to the people who read it. You must make readers care. Easy to say in nonfiction, right? Remember the parking lot memo? People who work for *The Boss* have a reason to care about where they park. But what about fiction? Can you make people care? Yes, you can. By the millions if you're good at it.

I don't mind saying it again: Check out the Amazon reviews and see just how much readers care about writing that lets them play along. Readers care when they *connect* with characters, story, images.

Let me ask you: Did you buy this book so you could help me make my mortgage payment? Or (*you can stop laughing now*) did you buy it because you care about selling your own novel? Can you dream about quitting your day job to write full-time, maybe travel to Italy to write your novel about the Emperor Nero?

Ah, so I did make you care. This book does matter to you. Translate that to your novel, as we see here in Janet Skeslien Charles's *Odessa*.

> I longed for love. For passion. For ecstasy. I knew what the words meant, but not how they *felt*. Love. Wasn't dancing in the Moonlight to music only two people hear? Was it washing socks and peeling potatoes? Was it sex? Was it tender? What were the exact ingredients? How do you make it grow? How do you kill it? How long do you have to suffer when it dies?

Love matters. To everyone. Here, Charles' heroine, Daria, is revealed in her quest for love, asking questions that you and I, if we don't already know the answers, care about knowing them.

TALES. This one is simple. Tell stories at every level of your writing. In words, phrases, sentences, paragraphs, Incidents. If you can tell story after story, layering your little stories into the big ones like cherries and chocolate under the black frosting of a devil's food cake, your readers will become the little children sitting jaw-dropped and white-eyed around the campfire at your feet, the chill of the dark woods on their bony backs. Your readers will turn one page and lick their fingers at once, already ready to go to the next. Because they're not leaving your story until you are done with it. They are in it. They are participants. Tales, tales, tales, even in the details, details, *de-tales*. This may be the sharpest tool in the toolbox.

This also might be a good place for me to mention your biggest battle in getting the attention of readers. The social media. Think about it. What is texting, e-mailing, blogging, posting, following? Answer: They are all forms of intimate participation. Each participation element can put you a step closer to stealing potential readers from the social media. This element alone, the idea of telling a tale every few words might stop those texting thumbs mid-word. If there's an area where Lee Child soars, this is it.

In this excerpt from *Gone Tomorrow*, Reacher is hiding out in the open, shopping in a supermarket. To look authentic…

> I developed a fantasy where I had an apartment nearby. I stocked its imaginary kitchen with enough stuff to last two whole days. Coffee, of course. Plus pancake mix, eggs, bacon, a loaf of bread … When I got bored and the basket got heavy I left it in a deserted aisle and slipped out the back of the store …

The narrator develops a fantasy and drags you into his imaginary kitchen. You have to ask yourself what you would stock for two days? He's making up a tale and dragging you briefly into it. Then he abandons his handbasket in a deserted aisle right where you can see it in your mind's eye—it's a great image, as well as a tiny tale.

IMAGERY. This is another arm-crossing trick on your brain. Don't call it description anymore. Description is what the hack writer does. He's the bus driver that stops the story right on the interstate to lecture riders about what they can see outside.

As a bus driver of a different kind and quality, you write images. The bus keeps moving, and the readers see a concrete, colorful, layered world that flows through their eyes and into their hearts. They see the herd of buffalo. They see the hunting party riding down on the herd on painted paint horses, white manes and black hair flying, spears and arrows at the ready.

From *Odessa*:

> Once, I invited an American missionary to my flat. When she stepped off the bus, she looked around and said, "It's like a cemetery. Look at all the gray tombstones sticking out of the ground." … afterward, I couldn't help but see my neighborhood through her eyes. Ugly. Gray. Dead. At my stop, I got off and on my way through the rusty kiosks and crude cement high-rises that hurt my soul to look at.

The term, gray tombstones, alone creates a fine image. But look at the craft. It's the missionary's observation, not the author's. And the narrator confirms it, then tells us how she feels about it. This is imagery at its best, imagery that counts because it has a huge, hurtful effect on the heroine.

CONFLICT. Donald Maass, author of *Writing the Breakout Novel*, has the best take ever on this one. Conflict dripping on every page is how he puts it. No best-seller ever became a best-seller without conflict. This includes *The Holy Bible*, all of the Harry Potter books, *The Three Little Pigs*, and *War and Peace*—even in the peaceful parts. If people hear an argument, they tune in to see what's going on. Even in a novel. *That's* participation. You can't ignore it.

In this Incident from *Odessa*, Daria interviews a well-dressed American seeking a wife at the social club where she works. By the way, the term, *snout*, means just what you think it means, *pig*.

> "I know a lot of the girls here. The more you tell me about what you desire in a spouse, the closer I can come to finding her."
>
> He surveyed the ballroom and said, "It's like a sea of breasts, thighs, and hair. And I'm the captain."

What a snout. He must have paid a lot because the Grande Dame was still circling. I gave her a pleading look and she responded by tightening her lips and narrowing her blue eyes.

"I like blondes," he said after a moment.

I rolled my eyes. Any woman could be a blonde.

No fist fights, not even a harsh word. But Daria is in conflict with two people here, one she does not even speak to. And the irony in that blonde remark, huh?

IRONY. A sense of humor. A witty character. A character telling a joke. the pathos implied when a senator would write a health care system and exempt himself from it. If you can make readers laugh at the wit in your story and marvel at the grand irony of it all, they will stick with you and overlook many of your other sins.

The people of Odessa live lives chock-full of irony, so Janet Skeslien Charles instills her heroine, Daria, with a supreme sense of irony.

Like many Odessans during Soviet times, my grandmother had to choose between luxuries like buying food and going to the dentist. (Philosophically, health care in the former Soviet Union was free. In practice, however, things were slightly different. You had to take a gift to the doctor. No gift, no treatment. No present, no future.)

Moments later Daria sees dried blood and spit in the sink because…

In Odessa, the city "conserved" water by turning it off during the day.

Later, Daria plays off her experience in this exchange:

Galya looked to me. "Have you ever trembled under a man's touch?"

"Yes, the dentist's."

PACING. Pacing is like the weather—everybody talks about it but nobody does anything about it. Until now. Pacing is an advanced writing tool that I introduced two books ago. It hasn't caught on the way I thought it should. So this time I'm going to build it into the system in layers. I'll teach you how to pick up the pace of your sentences and paragraphs with a simple and powerful tool that transcends gimmickry. We'll use it to sculpt the structure within an Incident and apply an advanced version of it to the entire novel.

You'll use it like spurs while riding the open range of Montana, riding down on a horse herd, aiming your camera, shooting dusky, dodgy, action images of mustangs in the stampede.

Do that and your readers will gallop across your pages trying to keep up. It's key to participation.

Go back to any of the reader review spots and notice how many times a reader will say that a novel's pace was too slow. Or in another novel where they report they were reading so fast they lost track of time. Then watch Lee Child at work here:

Lee Child's novels seldom lag. It's hard to choose a single well-paced segment from among so many in *Gone Tomorrow*. Here's one that has more than one element of participation.

> The square went quiet. There was a faulty letter in a lit-up sign to my left. It sputtered on and off at random intervals. I heard rats in the mulch behind me. I waited.
>
> Two minutes. Three.
>
> Then thirty-nine minutes into my forty I sensed human movement far to my right. Footfalls, disturbed air, holes in the darkness. I watched and saw figures moving through shadows and dim light.
>
> Seven men.
>
> Which was good news. The more now, the fewer later.

IMAGES. Action, even in the passage of time. Conflict. Short sentences and short paragraphs that add to ease of reading. Sight and sound. And that touch of irony in thinking it good news that seven men were coming at him. *Surprise.* All contributing to a quick pace. Could it be even quicker? Yes, with the fewest of tweaks. But let's not second-guess the author. Until later when we learn about pacing in detail.

ASPIRATIONS. By this I mean you should appeal to the goodness, justice, and fair play of people. I think that readers are especially good people. I think they want to be even better. I think they admire novels that uplift them, novels that appeal to their sense of justice because good wins out over evil. Abraham Lincoln called these aspirations the better angels of our nature. Even if readers cannot always achieve goodness themselves, they choose to live goodness through your characters. They really want good characters to do the right thing. So, believe in the goodness of your readers. And let them participate in the goodness of your novel by placing angels on one of their shoulders to contradict that evil spirit of the villain.

To use our two examples: Child makes Jack Reacher have a highly refined sense of justice who rewards the good folks and punishes the evil in all his travels.

Likewise, Janet Skeslien Charles writes Daria as a woman aspiring to achieve the Great American Dream by marrying into it and emigrating from Odessa. She creates even more irony when the aspirations don't work out—finding that you can't marry happiness? Remember the ending of the film, *Slumdog Millionaire*? All the characters dancing in the streets? Just in case you didn't get the ultimate feel-good feeling in this feel-good movie, the director leaves his audience with an upbeat message: *Let us dance in the aisles to celebrate the notion that goodness and love can triumph.*

TONE. This is the music, rhythm, voice, and song in your sentences. The element you've always known you should work on. And the one that has puzzled you when you find it lacking in a best-seller that the reviewers rave about. In a well-written story, every character sings a different song and the narrator has a voice of his own. They may harmonize. They may clash. Varying the tone can make a story sound real and feel chaotic or rough. Tone can cement all the aspects of a story into a symphony.

I used to think that this tonal music was the highest form of magic in writing. I still do admire it. But I also know that so many other factors help decide whether you get the most participation from readers. I know that some best-selling writers can succeed without it. I also know that you can do better if you can master it.

The writing sings on every page in *Odessa*, and here's just one example where the owner of the Internet matchmaker, Soviet Unions, gets excited about new ways to market women as brides to American husbands, know as the *social*, pronounced *soooo shall*. If you want to hear the music in it, read it aloud.

"*Soooo shall.* I haven't the slightest idea what it means. But it's our salvation."

She poured us both a *kognac* and described what she had seen, speaking so quickly the words bounced off my forehead. Men. Lots. Foreign. Rich. Women. Ours. Sexy. Young. Find mates. Expensive for men. Free for women. Music. Money. Alcohol. *Soooo shall.*

IDEAL. This refers to the Reading Ease Ideal (REI). This is the tool I invented a couple books ago to help writers edit their own work. The REI gives you a standard to use to revise with numeric goals in mind. First your computer counts words, characters, and lengths of sentences. It calculates reading level and instances of passive voice.

Then, using my REI goals, you edit your copy using shorter words, more concrete terms, shorter sentences, and active voice to revise your writing. You don't do this to suit me. You do it to suit your readers, so they need not labor in reading your novel. And, if you want to write longer sentences and use longer words or the passive voice to rewrite the music in your story, you are free to do so.

It's a three-step process that I will teach you. In short, the first step is to test your draft Incident against REI goals. The second step is to edit and re-edit that draft to meet REI goals. The third step is to revise your Incident to make it sing to your satisfaction, whether it meets the REI goals or not.

And, at the most advanced level in your writing, you will use one feature of this tool to help you pace each of your Incidents individually before going on to measure your overall story and adjust the intensity level at the proper points. You can elevate your novel's pace to best-seller status if you apply this tool well. And, no matter what kind of writer you are, you can elevate your own style to a whole new level.

I've tested dozens of novels against these REI goals. It's a given that the best-sellers usually meet or exceed standards that lesser novels rarely achieve.

ONLY TWO THOUSAND WORDS. I hit upon this idea while studying *The Presentation Secrets of Steve Jobs*, a book by Carmine Gallo. Gallo says that Jobs, whose presentations are legend, makes a drastic change in the tenor of his presentations every ten minutes. He switches to a video, for instance, or puts on a demo before going back to his present slides. Because even the most interested audience begins to get bored after ten minutes.

I ask you: *Why shouldn't writers do that in their books and novels?* In our age of Twitter and Facebook and endless random browsing, text messages, YouTube, and a thousand other distractions good and bad every hour of your life, your writing must compete.

I found research that says the average person reads at a pace of two hundred words a minute—and, by the way, unless you work at it, you haven't improved your reading pace since fifth grade. Sorry to be the one to tell you that. In any case, ten minutes at that pace is two thousand words. Frankly, I don't think you should even wait that long. But it's a heck of a tool to make you think every so often as you write. Put this tool in your toolbox. There's no rule to make you use it every two thousand words. But, like the other tools, just knowing it's there can give you a sense of comfort. Look, the more tools you have, the more options you have to add variety and to set your writing apart from the hack's.

NOVELTY. I think you already have a sense of this as a reader of novels yourself. Heck the word *novel* is in novelty. Notice how any hit sitcom springs from some new kind of character or situation. At least for a while. Soon three or four shows will ape the first one, bleeding its novelty, and somebody will have to come up with a new new idea. New words. New settings. New problems. I like teaching an old cliché new tricks every once in a while. That's a micronovelty. And I'm halfway through writing a new novel about a new problem that old baby boomers have to face, raising the parents who have raised them. Novelty on a large scale.

Readers love novelty. Readers and audiences certainly loved *Slumdog*. For one thing, they could play along with the quiz show. For another, you enjoy the deliciously novel idea that all those questions would reflect back on a real life.

SURPRISE. Surprise is as simple as a cliffhanger, a cameo appearance, an outcome not expected, a character killed off. Surprise goes beyond simple novelty because it has that snap to it in the shocking revelation, the twist. Surprise is novelty with attitude. It has to be brief: *sock, pow, oh wow!*

There's an element of surprise built into every chapter of a Lee Child novel. The opening line to the first chapter of *Gone Tomorrow* is six words long, remember:

> Suicide bombers are easy to spot.

The closing words:

> According to Israeli counterintelligence, I was looking at a suicide bomber.

QUESTIONS. Ask questions of your readers. I've asked a lot of questions in this edition of YCWAN. It's my way of getting you to participate in class. You can ask questions in novels, too. Your narrator can ask the rhetorical question, can't she? Your villain can ask your hero a question, say, *If you ever want to see your son alive, all you have to do is tell me. Where is the gold buried?* If your readers already know the burial spot, they're in on the secret and the danger. They're participating.

Questions form the basis of the entire dramatic story of both the novel and film, *Slumdog Millionaire*, in both the interrogation of Jamal and the questions he faces on the quiz show.

DIALOGUE. Dialogue is a way for readers to get into the story. Readers like to eavesdrop on conversations, in real life and in reading. So I have lots of suggestions on how to make your dialogue move fast. Force readers to listen in.

On another level your narrator of the novel should be conversational as she tells the story. The reader feels drawn in as a listener to the story is .

In *Odessa*, here's the owner of Soviet Unions again, talking to Daria:

> … I sank into my chair, relieved that she wasn't going to bring him up. Then she smirked and said, "I had no idea that having you full-time would bring such excitement. A date with Vladimir Stanislavsky?"
>
> "It's not a date. It's a walk. He's invited me to restaurants and to the opera, but I refused."
>
> "You love the opera. What's wrong with dating a young, handsome man?"
>
> "Who's an extortion king, mafia don, and possibly a killer?"
>
> "No one's perfect," she said. "At least he doesn't smoke."

A little bit of action and imagery. Lots of conflict apparent beneath the argument. And, again, the irony as a surprise ending to this tiny tale.

There you go. For a novelist, the list is life. If you go down the list and look at the first letters of each element, you find it reads: PARTICIPATIONSQD, which I have turned into a memory aid for myself: PARTICIPATIONS?"

I use it as a checklist. I have copies of it everywhere at work and at home. They say you're never farther than six feet from a spider. Maybe, maybe not. But I'm literally never farther than three feet from my checklist, which I've memorized, too. And which I've modified to use as a tool for writing Incidents and magazine stories and memos and PowerPoint presentations.

Some of these elements are more important than others, and we'll sort those out for special attention when we use it as a checklist to write Incidents.

For now, let's work with the first two incidents you've written.

DOES YOUR NOVEL HAVE WHAT IT TAKES TO SELL?

Keep that PARTICIPATIONS?" acronym at hand as we analyze your idea and the first two sketches you wrote in your first draft. Here we'll revisit that clearly bankable idea, *Slumdog Millionaire, analyzing its various elements.* As we do, you'll compare these elements to your own story. In fact, you'll get the chance here to measure your story so far against *Slumdog*. Don't be timid, either. *Slumdog* didn't begin as a multimillion dollar film. It began as an idea no better nor worse than the one you're noodling around right now.

And, for the record, that million-dollar idea was right out there in the open for any writer, including you or me, to jump on.

Now. Your idea.

Did You Identify an Idea That's Truly Salable?

All published novels begin with a salable idea.

Is your idea as commercial as the film *Slumdog Millionaire*? And did you know *Slumdog* was a novel before I told you? You didn't? Probably because its title was *Q&A* and it was written by Vikas Swarup. (After the film came out, the title on new editions became *Slumdog Millionaire*.) It's a good novel, and I liked it every bit as well as the film, although it's not quite the same story.

In any case, I think scriptwriters saw how to amp up the novel and really rang the bell with this one. Commercially, it is, I think, *The Perfect Story*.

As we shall see, from top to bottom, it has every element of participation that a story can take to the bank. Not to mention the huge bonus of the connection to the millionaire show everybody in the world has seen. *Slumdog Millionaire* is a high standard, but compare your idea to it anyway. Is *Slumdog* a lasting work of literary art? Decide that for yourself. It's not what we're talking about in this book. When I look at the story, both in film and in the novel, I find that the main character, Jamal, does not change very much from the opening to the closing of the story. And the reader/viewer is asked to suspend her disbelief. A lot. But I don't want to argue the point.

For now, forget all about agents, editors, and book buyers. Before you even consider them, you must test the salability of your idea on one very important person: you.

Can you sell your idea to *yourself*? Test your idea's salability by answering these questions:

- Do you feel such passion for the idea that you must write it into a novel?
- Do you believe you are the only person capable of telling the story the way it ought to be told?
- Can you sustain your excitement over the weeks or even months it may require to mold your idea into a finished novel?
- Can you make your story sound truly authentic? If not, are you willing to do the necessary research?

If you can answer yes to each of these questions, you've taken a huge first step toward making your novel salable. If an author doesn't believe in his own idea, there's little likelihood the book will ever get finished, let alone published.

Where did you get your idea?

1. **Did you steal from existing stories?** Putting a new spin on existing ideas is risky for two reasons: (1) chances are that somebody else is already doing such a story; (2) cycles of popularity end without warning. You're better off starting with something fresh. You might put in a year of work and try to hit the market at the same time as hundreds of other writers, some of them pros. Above all, don't steal from television—most of the jaded ideas there have been stolen from other TV shows, many more than once.

2. **Did you borrow from current events?** Stealing actual events from the national news is probably not salable unless you're Dominick Dunne. If it's in the news, some novelist with a track record is already phoning her agent. Or unless you can pull off something as inventive as Vikas Swarup, author of the novel renamed *Slumdog Millionaire.*

TEST YOUR IDEA AGAINST REALITY: A QUIZ

Let's analyze your first two sketches and put your darling idea to a test of fire. You must be ruthless, because if you don't hold an idea to strict standards at this early stage of your novel, it might falter, withering after you've put in weeks of labor. So be tough on that idea now and spare yourself later grief.

Speaking of realities, here are the two salient realities about publishing:

First, as a rule, it's all business. No one in the business cares about you or your Great American Novel unless he thinks one or both of you can make money for him. It's that element of relevance in participation. If people think you can make money for them, they care. If they think you can make a lot of money for them, they *really* care.

Second, next to money, time is the most important commodity in publishing. As you put together your novel, it's also a good idea to begin formulating a plan for marketing it without wasting an editor's or agent's time.

The Essential Elements of a Salable Novel

Rate your idea on a scale from 1 to 10 on each of the following:

1. DOES YOUR NOVEL IDEA FEATURE A TRULY HEROIC CHARACTER? Is your heroic character (often called the lead or protagonist) energetic, morally upright, fair, and likable? Does she always strive to do the right thing, even if her judgment is flawed? Is she kind to friends, dogs, and old ladies, and stalwart against injustice? Is she unique, transcending every stereotype you've seen on television and in the movies? Is she striking in a way other than her physical attributes? Think about that heroic kid, Jamal, in *Slumdog*. Honest, earnest, smart, funny. Above all, a romantic hero rising out of a world of squalor.

1 is Mediocre ————————————— 10 is Breathtakingly Heroic

Your heroic character rates _____.

2. DOES YOUR HERO HAVE A WORTHY GOAL? Heroic characters must be *for* something substantially good and *against* all things evil, yet they ought to struggle with both. How strongly does such a goal matter to the character and to the reader? The film's *Slumdog* hero wasn't in it for the money. He was in it for love. The money was simply an object to help him earn Latika's love. In the novel, there's another mystery quest as well. But you don't even learn about that until the story is virtually over. So it hardly matters here, and I won't spoil the plot for you. Measure your hero on a scale of 1 to 10.

1 is Trivial ————————————10 is Heroically Worthy

Your heroic character's goal rates _____.

3. DOES YOUR HERO HAVE A WORTHY ADVERSARY? Adversary, villain, nemesis, antagonist, antihero, obstacle—you get the idea. Whether the heroic character is fighting velociraptors, mobsters, natural disasters, alien visitors, or fatal personal errors, is she constantly thrown up against impossible odds? What's the toughness of the competition? In *Slumdog* the cast of characters standing in the way of our hero's quest was a lineup worthy of a superhero. The slum. The caste system. Organized crime. Ordinary criminals. Extraordinary criminals. Police. The game show. Poverty. Religion. The weather. Bugs. Disease. Every day a fight for survival.

1 is Cream Puff ————————————10 is Heroically Worthy

Your heroic character's adversary rates _____.

4. DOES YOUR IDEA EMBODY PLENTIFUL ACTION AND CONFLICT? We're not simply talking car chases and explosions, riots, shootings, and all the other action and conflict, latent and obvious, in *Slumdog*. Rather, do you envision a novel packed with descriptions of static situations, or does it come alive with clashes—personal, internal, external, and eternal? Do characters interact rather than muse incessantly? Does the story move toward a conclusion? What's the pace of your novel?

> 1 is Catatonic ————————————10 is Heroically Animated

> Your novel's activity level rates _____ .

5. DO YOU ALREADY HAVE A HEROIC ENDING IN MIND? The ending includes a final epic struggle between your heroic character and her worthy adversary. Have you planned a powerful physical, emotional, or mental dilemma that will be resolved in the heroic character's favor? Does she learn a lesson that is worthwhile and meaningful to the rest of us mortals? How compelling is your ending? Did you feel like standing up and dancing in the aisles with the film's cast after watching the film *Slumdog Millionaire*? I did.

> 1 is "So what?" —————————————————10 is Heroic

> Your novel's ending rates _____.

Scoring Your Idea

Let's compare your idea's score to a few criteria that add to or diminish your total.

The Heroic Character

If you didn't start with an 8 or a 9, you don't yet have a character worth reading about. Stop right here and go back to square one. Either come up with a fresh idea or revise your heroic character. Same deal if you scored this element a 10. Perfect characters aren't as believable as ones with flaws and an Achilles heel—even Superman has his kryptonite. Add a fatal flaw to your main character so the reader can more easily identify with her. Give her a weakness so crucial that if she succumbs to it, she's in danger of destroying herself. She might be a recovering alcoholic, for example. Once your character is flawed, add 5 points, bringing your total to 13 or 14.

However, if, as in Kathryn Stockett's *The Help*, you have multiple heroic characters who narrate and share the load of carrying the story, subtract 2 points for a second main character, 3 for a third, and so on. If you have as many main characters as the film *The Big Chill*, you'll end up with a score below zero. Yes, I know that Ms. Stockett's novel was a first effort. Consider that she had a job at a publishing house in New York. Imagine that she knew people who would buy her novel. If you have such a step up, by all means give it a try. If you don't, I suggest you not risk it until your second or third novel.

If your heroic character has a love interest, add 3 points. Romance sells novels, even in so-called "boy books," where it's sometimes called sex.

If your heroine has a unique career or rare view of life, add a point for each. If she has a wry sense of humor, add 5 points. If that sense of humor is too smart-alecky, like mine, subtract 3. Something I always have to do.

If your hero dies at the end of the book, subtract 59 points for using such poor judgment as a first novelist. Don't cite the character Gus in *Lonesome Dove* unless you're Larry McMurtry himself. Just start all over again. Sell your book, then ask the editor if you can kill your heroine.

When you've finished calculating, your score should be no less than sixteen, no more than 24. Anywhere in that range gives you a heroic character that you can work with.

Your Character's Goal

If it isn't in the range of 8 to 10, elevate it somehow. The heroine must strive for more than obtaining the perfect parking space, like George Costanza on *Seinfeld*. The reader ought to care about what a heroic character is battling for or against. If you rated the goal a 10, which is out of reach to most people, give yourself a bonus of 2; but, if the goal you set seems impossible, give yourself a 5 instead. Worry about writing out of that impossible situation later. You can't make things too hard on a heroic character if you want to sell your novel. Your score on this element should now be between 10 and 15. If it's lower, reconsider the toughness of the goal. If it's higher, I admire your imagination, if not your math. Let it stand.

Your Character's Adversary

If the antagonist isn't rated 8 or 9, your heroic character might not be challenged. If you gave your adversary a higher starting score than your main character, add 2 points for envisioning extreme difficulties. But if you gave the antihero a 10, subtract 2. Don't create a villain with no saving graces. Even the most vile adversary ought to at least be kind to his mother.

Avoiding the pitfalls I've pointed out, redefine your concept of an adversary until the adjusted score ranges from 10 to 11.

Your Story's Action and Conflict

If you don't envision a novel with a pace equal to a range of 8 to 10, you might as well be writing a phone book. Every scene should be filled with tension and action. Keep description to a minimum—in the hands of an amateur, it can induce reader narcolepsy.

UCLA professor Richard Walter, author of *Screenwriting: The Art, Craft, and Business of Film and Television Writing*, wrote screenwriting's lone unbreakable rule: "Don't be boring." My take on that succinct advice: *Never be boring, not for one scene, paragraph, sentence, or word. Every writing rule in the book has an exception—except for this one.*

Your Ending, the Closer

You've already sketched your Closer, right? If not, now is the time.

Your Closer must be even more powerful than the Opener. Add 3 points if you have imagined a climactic scene as the zenith of action and excitement for your novel, even more important than your Opener. If your heroic character comes away unscathed, subtract 2, for that's a fairy tale. If she is scarred but wiser for the experience, add 2. If the villain is not vanquished, subtract 3. If the outcome of your novel is decided by a coincidence, act of God, or quirky force or new character who jumps into the novel at the last moment, subtract 99 points from your score and start over. Your hero alone and no outside cavalry can determine the outcome of a salable novel. In the end, you should have a score of 14 or higher.

Final Scoring

When you've finished this exercise, you must have the minimum score for each element. It doesn't matter what the total numbers are because every individual area must be strong. Nothing much matters for the other elements if your main character is a repulsive slug of a man and a serial rapist besides. Not even John Updike could make a hero out of such a soul. If you want to quote Dexter, the heroic(?) serial killer from the TV show (adapted from the novels that began with *Dearly Devoted Dexter* by Jeff Lindsay) back at me, go ahead. I found the story fascinating for a while. But troubling. And I don't recommend trying to break into selling by following such a bizarre course.

The reality for a first novelist is this: *If you don't envision a truly heroic character with heroic goals on an action-packed journey, encountering obstacles and a worthy opponent, and arriving alive and wiser at the end of your novel after having engaged in a titanic struggle, it's not likely your novel will be seriously considered in the publishing business.*

I'm thinking serial killers need not apply. Noodle your idea until you meet that standard.

REFINE YOUR IDEA INTO A WRITTEN NUGGET STATEMENT

State your idea in no more than thirty-five to forty words. This is practically done for you if you've faithfully tested your idea against reality in the previous step. The point of this exercise is to condense your novel idea. A nugget contains these elements:

YOUR WORKING TITLE. The nugget needs a title. It helps you focus your project. If you don't have one yet, we'll develop that first thing in the next chapter (see page 43). But if you must skip ahead, do that now, and come back here to finish your nugget after you've found your working title.

YOUR CATEGORY OR TOPIC. This should be stated in two words or phrases, tops. Is your story a romance, comedy, or romantic comedy? Is it a thriller, a crime thriller, a techno-thriller, a mystery, a fantasy, an action-adventure, a Western, science fiction, horror, a coming-of-age story, or something else? What category would define your intended work? If you can't identify a category, look over the list in *Writer's Market*, or check out the genres, complete with best-seller lists, on Amazon.

Caution: Stick to one or two genres only, please. You should not submit a romance/science-fiction/crime/thriller/Western unless you feel compelled to reveal yourself as an amateur.

YOUR SKETCH OF THE NOVEL. Your entire story should be packed on the little backs of only thirty-five to forty words.

Here's an example from the film version of …

> *Slumdog Millionaire*: **Rags-to-Riches Romance**
>
> Gritty drama of an Indian slum boy winning on *Who Wants to Be a Millionaire?* He draws on a horrid life to answer questions on the show, and unfolds his quest to rescue his lifelong love from the clutches of evil.

Forty words, not counting the title and category. What's explicit in that very short story?

- **The heroic character**—the slum boy, Jamal in the film.

- **The central issue of the story (plotline).** In his quest to win the love of his life, Latika, Jamal stays just one step ahead of police, criminals, his brother, poverty—everything in the world that is against him—all of it framed within the context of his appearances on a national quiz show. In the novel, the writer stated explicitly in this line of dialogue: *"Well, wasn't I lucky that they asked only those questions to which I knew the answers?"*

- **The heroic goal**—to win the love of Latika. Notice: It's not about the millions. It's all about love. But just in case you're not that romantic, there are those millions.

- **The worthy adversary.** This hardly overstates it: All the evil in the world, which we learn includes Jamal's own brother, big evils like poverty and prejudice and organized crime, as well as a society that is against him, and the game show host. And let's not forget the little evils, as well, like family, thugs, and rats.

- **Action**—in the suggestions of battle and rescue from evil.

- **The ending**—triumph over evil is implied.

As a bonus, the forty words include:

- **A grabber**—coming out of the slums to win millions on a game show. That's a novelty, all right.

- **A twist**—the story of his life told in questions on the game show.

WRITE YOUR NUGGET

Now write a nugget based on your idea for a novel. Include all of these elements and more, if you wish. Here are some tips to help you get started:

- Write as if telling a best friend about a movie you have just seen.

- Don't worry about word count the first time through. Just get it down. Address all the elements of a salable idea and as many principles of participation as you can.

- Use specific present-tense verbs that describe the action as if it is happening in the here and now. The example uses *fights*, *trap*, *rescues*, and *erases*.

- Use precise nouns.

- Tighten. Don't stop refining this until you get to thirty-five to forty words. Fewer words means you're leaving out a possible grabber. More means you're not working at it.

How about your own nugget? Got it done? Great. Remember, you can change it as we go along. A chapter from now, if you feel a sudden urge to change your idea, go right ahead. Modify your first Nugget right in the middle of your novel, or select a new one.

POSITION YOUR IDEA WHERE YOU CAN SEE IT

Type or print your idea onto 3" × 5" (8cm × 13cm) note cards. Carry one in the pocket of your pants or shirt. Put another one in the place where you'll be writing your novel. Stick another on the visor of your car. Carry one in your planner. Keep this nugget in front of you at all times as a reminder of your novel and the story you want to tell. The nugget will hold your focus and set the limits of the topic, keeping you on track until you write "The End."

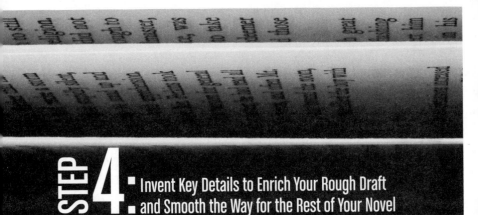

> *Have a little fun as you begin to solidify your novel. Add some of the easy pieces.*
>
> Here's what you're going to do in chapter 4.
>
> - Refine a working title.
> - Add a digital cast of characters.
> - Select names for your characters.
> - Adopt a point of view.

CHOOSE A WORKING TITLE

A good title works magic on books and films. Somebody utters the title *Jaws*, still one of the best ever, and an image forms in your mind at once, vivid and toothy. You've probably already chosen a title. If so, rag on it like a puppy on a rawhide bone. Maybe you'll improve it.

In his book *How to Write Best Selling Fiction*, Dean Koontz says the five things that influence somebody to buy a book are: (1) a proven author's name; (2) the subject matter of the novel; (3) the cover art; (4) the influence of the ad copy on the cover; (5) a quick reading of the first page. I would add (6) the title.

A grabber title can, at least for that brief first glance, snag the attention of an agent or editor who receives your pitch. Editors and agents are word people. If your title snaps its fingers at them from your pitch letter, the title has done its job. Not to mention it might catch the eye of a shopper who's browsing the shelves or Web pages.

A great title also inspires great cover art in the Dean Koontz list. Together, title and art can induce an impulse buyer to pick up your novel from the book table and read that first page and the ad copy on the covers.

I think *Slumdog Millionaire* works far better as a title than *Q&A*, don't you? Let's talk about your title.

Is your working title short and snappy? As a rule, snappy titles give a book commercial appeal. Editors, reviewers, sellers, and critics prefer a short handle when talking about your novel. Also, short titles fit best on a book's spine.

Exceptions? Yes. *The Girl with the Dragon Tattoo* and *Harry Potter and the Half-Blood Prince*. Don't we wish those long titles belonged to our novels and royalty payments?

Does your title position your book? It should be clear to editors, agents, ad staff, booksellers, and book buyers what category your book fits in or what topic you'll be addressing. *The Six-Gun Kid* suggests one thing, and *A Virtuous Woman* something else.

Does your title lend itself to cover artwork? It's hard to beat *Jaws*, isn't it? *The Help*? It's hard to imagine cover art for Kathryn Stockett's novel. *Shutter Island* falls in between the two, with a picture of an Alcatraz-like place and Leonardo DiCaprio on the cover and that wonderful advertising tagline that every novelist dreams of: *Now a Major Motion Picture.*

Finally, remember this about good titles: *A good title is what your publisher says it is.* Many best-selling authors have title approval in their contracts. Experts and celebrities can capitalize on their power to insist on titles for their books. All you have is the power of persuasion.

Your publishing house knows more than you or me about selling books. If they insist on a title change, give in.

For it's more important that you write such a terrific story that it sells into the land of "Now a Major Motion Picture." That way you can have the image of a celebrity on *your* cover.

COLLECT A GALLERY OF CHARACTERS

Time for a little fun using a trick I learned from my friend, novelist R. Karl Largent. Untie that bundle of old *New York Times Magazines* in the garage and launch your own character hunt. Clip and rip, gathering bodies and faces to use in casting your novel. Look for photos of the famous, the near famous, and the unknown model whose portrait is used to sell everything from eye shadow to nasal hair clippers.

When you go to the doctor, dentist, barber, or hairdresser, page through the magazines. Should you run across a character with character—any age, gender, or race—do one of two things: Either run to the newsstand and buy that issue of the magazine so you can collect the character for your gallery or rip the heart from the magazine right there in the waiting room. Your decision is between you, your conscience, and your hairdresser.

Gather the family photo albums and find the most interesting faces there. Drag out the high school yearbook. Collecting people you know lets you borrow personality traits as well as physical ones.

Do searches online. Print images of people from Websites. Search for a site that is somehow related to your novel's topic and see if there are any pictures of people on the site or in ads on the site. They may fit your needs perfectly.

Store the pictures in a box or folder. When a character enters your novel, find the picture that suits her and transfer her from your gallery to your cast of characters (either a folder or a digital picture file).

Using an actual picture helps when you create the word picture of your hero. You pull up the photo and tell what you see there. When I write a novel, I plaster the walls with pictures of my cast. It's one of those times when hard copy works better for me than bits and bytes.

Bonus Idea—picture your settings as well.

Use this same trick to collect beaches and jungles, deserts and forests, cityscapes and national parks for your novel (*National Geographic*), fashions (*GQ*, *Vogue*), and so on.

Casting Cautions

- **Caution one:** Don't collect only the beautiful. Gather people with glasses as well as contact lenses. Find all shades of skin and hair color. Look for the fat, the thin, the smooth, and the rough. Find men with beards and women with mustaches. Search out warts, triple chins, crooked teeth, bald heads, and wild hair. In short, create a realistic world of characters. The novel packed with nothing but pretty people is too much to be believed.

- **Caution two:** You may find it helpful to use photos of the famous and familiar but don't identify them. Don't say your character has "Paul Newman eyes." Give your hero an original persona. Along with this goes the warning to avoid describing Aunt Bertha right down to the identifying "Born to raise hell" tattoo across her nose. You wouldn't want to hurt Aunt Bertha's feelings—or to have her hurt yours.

- **Caution three:** Don't get hung up on collecting characters. Sure, it's a fun activity, but it won't get your novel written. Keep moving.

CREATE A DIRECTORY OF CHARACTER NAMES

Naming characters is also fun—except when you find yourself all wrapped up in writing a hot scene and a new character crashes the story. You won't want to stop writing to invent a name. Better to have a list of names filed away and ready to use. Here's how to build your own ready-to-use name directory:

COLLECT SOME INTERESTING LAST NAMES. Divide a sheet of paper or text file into three columns and label it like this:

Name Directory

Last Names	Male Names	Female Names

Open a phone book to the *A* listings. Copy some last names into the first column of your name directory. Collect three to five last names that begin with *A*. Use names that you react to. You like them. You dislike them. They sound good when you say them aloud.

Do the same for listings from *B* to *Z*. Don't worry if you have trouble finding names that begin with *Q*, *U*, *X*, and *Z*. You may get only one or two. No problem. Just go on to the next letter.

COLLECT SOME INTERESTING FIRST NAMES AT RANDOM. Pick any page in the phone book, and write down the best male and female first names you find. Fill the last two columns of your directory with these names. **Caution:** Do not put the real first names of people with their real last names.

When it comes time to build some names for your heroic characters, choose a last name you like from the directory. Then choose a first name that goes with it. Say the full name aloud to see if it sounds all right. Choose a middle name as well, if you like. Each time you select a name and write it into your character file, cross it off the worksheet or mark it on the digital file so you won't use it again.

File your faces and names together.

A Checklist for Your Name Directory

- **Don't use names of real people, even if you're trying to be kind to your friends.** You might insult somebody who misreads your intended compliment. What's more, people who wish to keep their lives private don't like reading stories about themselves, even true ones.

- **Don't use names that sound like the names of real people or somebody else's characters.** Sorry, you can't get around the first "don't" by moving a few letters around in the name. If you insulted a character named Clillary Hinton, we'd know.

- **Don't use names that might be confused with famous fictional characters, either.** Clark Kent would be a lousy name for one of your characters, and you could be sued for using it. Worse, you'd be guilty of a far more heinous crime: being boring. You can do better than that.

- **Don't use names that sound alike.** This is a "don't" that has six shades to consider:

  1. Avoid names that begin with the same letter. Darwin, Dewey, and Del. Too confusing.

  2. Avoid names that can be both masculine and feminine. Eliminate Pat, Terry, Robin, and Bobby unless you want to confuse identities to create a twist.

  3. Be wary of names that could be either first or last names, such as Grant or Tyler or James or Kelly or Chase or Wilson. You can use them, but be aware of the potential for confusion—Kathryn James, a woman you call James when you use her last name in the story.

  4. Don't overuse alliteration, that is, first and last names that begin with the same letter. Bobby Burns, Todd Trotter, and Kay Kaufman in the same story? Too much.

  5. Don't use names that sound like half the people in the phone book. Mary Jones? Bill Johnson? Try to be more creative than that (at least for your character's sake). And never use Jim Smith—it's my name and way too common already.

  6. And don't use names that rhyme in the same story. A group of people with the names Bill, Gil, Jill, Lil, and Phil just isn't pretty.

- **Be wary of long names.** Imagine a hero Augustine Degaetanis. You'd get exhausted just typing Degaetanis a thousand times. That's not to say you can't use long names. Just don't be too hard on yourself.

- **Be conscious of names ending in *s*.** This might seem like a strange one, but just think about it for a minute. Using names that end in *s* can cause awkward punctuation when you want to show possession. Suppose your heroic character is Iris James. Whatever she possesses is Iris's. When two or more members of her family appear in a scene, they are the Jameses. Their house is the Jameses', which is enough to make you avoid such names altogether.

- **Don't be too cute.** Doris B. Goode? Maybe in a kid's storybook, but nowhere else.

- **Don't use a name twice.** Remember to cross a name off your name directory when you transfer it to your character sheet. You don't want to risk confusing your readers or yourself.

DEVELOP YOUR CHARACTER KIT

You have your names. You had your faces. Let's put them together.

Characters in your novel come in three categories: master characters, major characters, and minor characters.

Master Characters Go to the Top of Your List

Master characters drive the story. By their personalities, behavior, and decisions, they dictate the action, timing, direction, and pace of your novel. They are usually the:

- Hero or heroine (protagonist, heroic character)
- Villain (antagonist, heroic character's adversary)
- Lover (heroic character's love interest, main squeeze)

They are the Clark Kent, Lex Luthor, and Lois Lane of your novel. You ought to give them faces and personalities as striking as their duties in carrying your novel on their backs.

You can find any number of novels in which there is no love interest. Maybe you will write and sell one. All I'm saying here is that, if you can get wider participation in your story by using the power of romance, why wouldn't you? Men and women alike mostly do aspire to be in love. Love is the one great emotion that everybody cares about.

Now. If you're novel's antagonist is a force of nature, as the sea was in *The Perfect Storm*, treat it like a master character. In *The Help*, I think you could treat the racism of the civil rights era as a compelling antagonist as well. So give that a master character entry as well. The Ku Klux Klan is a faceless group antagonist in the same story, and you could easily treat it as a Master character as well.

Major Characters Are Next

Major characters help master characters drive the story. They are the Perry White and Jimmy Olsen to your Lois and Clark. They make decisions within the story's context, but they seldom dictate the outcome of important events. As a rule, only master characters do that in salable novels. Select unique pictures for these characters as well.

Minor Characters Fall Below the Others

Minor characters are all your extras. They're the walk-ons, the cabdrivers, the fat uncles, and loony aunts of your master and major characters. But don't create stereotypes. Invent unique people even if they're not rounded as fully as the more important players.

With a bit of luck and a lot of craft on your part, all your master and major characters will assume lives of their own. Readers love this type of character better than any artificial, two-dimensional type. In fact, such characters can become unruly as their natures develop throughout their story. What's more, as the cast fills out, the sheer number of new characters may overwhelm, making it very difficult to keep them straight in your mind. Not to mention the mountain of personal detail that shape your characters throughout the novel, which can be immense.

My digital casting system will solve the problem.

A DIGITAL WRITER'S TOOLKIT TO KEEP TRACK OF CHARACTERS

Instead of cards and paper, I now use a digital system for keeping track of characters and Incidents. You can download all or part of it free from my Website www.writefromparadise.com. Whatever system you choose to use, your kit can save you hours of time wasted in duplication of effort and flat-out boneheaded mistakes.

I used to track master, major, and minor characters separately. No more. Now they're all in the same digital file. Characters getting the most work in the story stay at the top of the digital list. If a minor player blossoms, he moves up. If somebody dies or or plays a lesser role, she moves down. Sorting is never more than a couple keystrokes or mouse clicks away. It's just that easy because I work in the Outline View of Microsoft Word, which allows you to collapse all the character traits so that all you see is a list of names and roles. Each time I review a character I expand only his entry in the file.

How to Build Your Novel's Digital Cast File

Download the template, Digital_Cast_Masterfile from my site www.*writefromparadise.com*. Before you do anything else, create a copy of the file and rename it, using the title of your novel (for example: *Cast of Characters for Sharks*). That way, you'll always have the master file to go back to and copy from.

Switch to Outline under the View feature in Word. After you do, your screen will look something like this.

⊹ Name of Character 1 (Hero) Age:

⊹ Name of Character 2 (Villain) Age:

⊹ Name of Character 3 (Lover) Age:

⊹ Next Character ( ) Age:

⊹ Next Character ( ) Age:

⊹ Next Character ( ) Age:

The Outline View hides everything except the names of characters, their roles in your novel, and the character's age.

Each of those lines will expand to reveal space for a full dossier. Double-click on the plus sign to the left of your main character, and you get this:

Name of Character 1 (Hero) Age:
Arc (How will this character and attitude change?)
A
D
Z

Goals and motivation:
Mission-duty:
Career-selfish:
Romance-sexual:
Quirks:
Fatal Flaw:
Saving grace:
Voice, Word Choice:
Pertinent bio and Relevant backstory:

> Looks
> Hair
> Eyes
> Nose
> Mouth
> Hands
> Striking feature

Caution: Before you begin work, make space for more characters.

Select Outline under View in the main menu. Then, in the task bar with all the green arrows near the center of the screen you should see the words, "Show Level 1." If you see a blank space in the center of the screen on that bar, click the tiny black upside down pyramid and select the words, "Show Level 1." That collapses everything but the heading for names of your cast.

Once you're in the Level 1 mode, highlight and copy the last three lines from your template, which look like this:

✛ Next Character ( ) Age:

✛ Next Character ( ) Age:

✛ Next Character ( ) Age:

Once you've copied those lines, place the cursor at the end of the file. Add a return. Paste from the clipboard at least three or four times. That will add nine or twelve blank dossiers for your cast. Do this as many times as you like if you have your own *War and Peace* going. Later, if you fill out the last cast member, you can always scroll back to the master file and copy the last three dossiers, again in outline view, and paste them back into your novel's cast.

Now you can begin building your cast.

Highlight the words, "Name of Character 1," and type your hero or heroine's name. Just like that, you're on your way. Do the same for each character you know. If you also know what your character looks like, double-click on that plus sign beside the name to expand the dossier. Place your cursor in after the word, *hair* under *Looks*, for instance.

You might type: *This guy's hair looks like greasy, grimy gopher guts, brown, shaded to green, coarse as shag carpet matted with gum.* There now. If at any time during the writing of your story you mention that the character has blond, curly locks, but then you think that doesn't sound quite right, it's easy to check it out. Just double-click on the plus sign beside that character's name and the dossier will expand to show the gopher guts detail.

Before you start work on a new character, double-click on the plus sign before the name of the character you've finished with, and that will collapse all the information and clean up your screen. Then double-click on the next character and get to work. When you're finished, come back here so I can tell you what the other terms mean to me.

I've included a short course in using Outline View on my Website and Microsoft Word provides many more details under Help in the program.

CHARACTER ARC

Let's talk about something new. I've added the term *character arc* to the cast dossier, so you could consider how each character might change over the course of your story. And this applies, I think, to minor characters as well as major ones. A member of the cast of your novel should learn something between the opening Incident and the Closer. The more your characters learn, the more your readers learn. The more your readers learn, the more they participate. Think of this like the arrows in the diagram below. In this case in the Opener, A, as she enters the story a cast member is one way. Along the way of the novel, something happens, in this case our PoNRI. The woman changes and begins to evolve along the way. This is not to specify a particular point at which a change should happen. Only a suggestion of how it might happen in the case of one character.

In the character dossier for each character, I've placed these three points as headings. You may change them as you please. You may add more points as a cast member undergoes several changes. My intention is to give you a starting point which, as I say, looks like this:

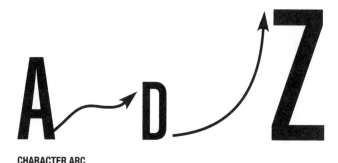

SKETCH OUT AT LEAST THREE MASTER CHARACTERS

Your master characters must sell your novel every bit as much as your sizzling plot and intriguing synopsis have to. That's why we're going to spend so much time with them in this step.

Your novel plays out in relation to the world of your hero. If an action, setting, or other character does not relate to the hero—either as a cause or an effect—odds are that action, setting, or character doesn't belong in the novel.

If you focus on your heroine's universe and derive your story from it as a starting point, enlarge it, dramatize it, and follow it consistently to the ending, you simplify the job of writing. Your final draft will have unity, coherence, and all those other elements you barely remember from your literature classes.

Think of your novel in terms of a hero's universe clashing with a villain's universe and you will have distilled the business of writing a novel to its essence.

Let's fill in some of the blanks on your cast of characters.

Writing Your First Character

With the Digital Cast open, let us breathe life into a character. Open the top character entry fully to show all levels, that is, all headings.

ENTER NAMES ON THE FIRST LINE. When a new person walks into your story, give her a name using your new name directory. Put any nicknames in quotation marks, and if you base the character on a real person, you might want to write that in parentheses so you don't forget.

Identify the role the character plays in the story (CEO, pilot, drifter, supermodel, supermom, psychic, vampire, heroine, detective, whatever) and her age.

UNDER ARC TELL HOW THE HERO WILL CHANGE AT POINTS IN YOUR NOVEL. Remember, the best stories are the ones in which most characters change the most. Beside each of the letters, ADZ, write a sketch, a few words will do, about changes, especially attitude changes that the character will undergo through the story. At A, you should tell where your hero is at the Opener. At B, how he might change. At C, how he would end the story. Be brief. If he changes more than once, add another letter, say a W.

COMPLETE THE "PHYSICAL" SECTION. Look at her picture. Visualize the rest of her. If your hero's eye color is blue in the opener of your novel, you don't want them to go brown midway through your novel, unless he's using colored contact lenses as a disguise.

Perhaps the most important box in the physical section, though, is "Striking Features." Think about it. Everybody is memorable in some way—either size, beauty, ears, or one of the other features listed on the sheet. Here you note the character's signature features. A feature can become a tag by which a reader identifies the character. Quasimodo had his hunched back in *The Hunchback of Notre Dame*, and in Tom Robbins's novel, *Even Cowgirls Get the Blues*, Sissy Hankshaw had thumbs as long as jumbo hot dogs. A striking attribute makes for striking imagery, but far more than that within the story a character reacts to his striking feature in one or more ways, and other characters react in a variety of ways, which enriches a story.

Quasimodo's hunchback made him a recluse so he could avoid being mocked, but Sissy Hankshaw idolized her oversized thumbs and exploited them all her life. Other characters in those tales reveal their natures—cruel, curious, kind, and the like—in the ways they react to the hunchback and the thumbs.

You needn't create extremes to make a striking feature work. You're better off drawing intricate personalities instead of cartoon exteriors.

Now, here's a point that flies in the face of all I've told you so far: Elmore Leonard has a rule in his list of 10 Rules of Writing. Number 8 is: *Avoid detailed descriptions of characters.*

Mr. Leonard quotes a character from John Steinbeck's novel *Sweet Thursday*:

> "I like a lot of talk in a book and I don't like to have nobody tell me what the guy that's talking looks like. I want to figure out what he looks like from the way he talks."

I read a lot of Elmore Leonard novels, and I like his style. Literally. But I'm not as adamant as he is on this point and don't want to push it on you. Hey, not everybody can write like Leonard. He's a screenwriter, too, a world that uses quick and dirty strokes to paint an image of a character. It would be a waste of time to write in a fat and greasy white gangster, when the producers are trying to get Denzel Washington for the part.

I like to think of character imagery as a participation issue. Use as few words as you can, selecting words that pack the max color, to splash an image on canvas. If you resist the urge to paint every hair on the hero's head, the reader will do the job well enough.

So sketch with broad strokes, dial up the imagery on a few main points, and leave room for a reader to play a part in your novel. Don't try to rule a reader's brain. The trick is to give her mind a shove. Then stand back and let her mind ramble on its own.

WRITE A BRIEF "PERTINENT BIO." This is a danger zone. Don't overwrite here. I used to use 5" × 8" (13cm × 20cm) cards as character cards in my writer's toolkit. The lack of space to write a bio was a plus. A few square inches to sketch out an entire life story. I wanted to squelch the temptation to write bulky bios. Now you have a text file with endless space. But be strong and be spare. Limit yourself to a few headlines and main points, if you will, and keep to fewer than one hundred words. Then expand your ideas when you flesh out your novel.

You can always tell when a writer has done endless research and feels compelled to include it all in the text. Those are the parts you skip to get back to the story. And it happens to the best-sellers, too.

This file is a working document, a place to record notes and new ideas. Later, as your story and characters develop, more ideas will occur to you. Write the new facts and insights right into the story and make a note in the proper section of the dossier. I use keywords in both files. Suppose three chapters in, your villain has his mother's name, Rosalie, tattooed on your hero's left earlobe. After the day's writing, you update your dossier to include the Rosalie tattoo. If you ever need to revisit that place in chapter 3, you can check the dossier, refer to the keyword, and use it as a search term under the *Find* feature in the main text file.

NOTE THE "VOICE, WORD CHOICE" SECTION OF THE SHEET. In the world outside a novel, you read people daily in a hundred different ways. You can spot the one-of-a-kind eyebrows of your lover in a crowd of thousands at the ball game. A wink, a wave, a way of walking—one glimpse of a face or gesture and you know a friend's mood.

Do the same with each character's voice and word choice.

What does your boss unfailingly say when she's giving one of those "things are going to have to change around here" speeches? Does she open with, "People?" When handled well, a reader will know who's speaking in your novel even if the author doesn't attribute every spoken line.

Each time a character uses a fresh word, go to "Voice, Word Choice" section and make note of the word, expression, or vocal tic. Later, you can refer to his sheet so you can remain true to the character and perhaps even enrich him in every Incident.

Vocal Dos and Don'ts:

Don't write dialects. Readers don't like dialects, and editors hate them. Reasons enough to avoid writing them. Not to mention the chance of offending a racial or social minority. Better to hint at a dialect. For example: "Whatchoo gunna do 'bout it, mistuh?" is far inferior to "What are you gun do about it, mister?" in which only one word hints at the voice. Let the reader supply meaning to speech patterns. For a great example, see Kathryn Stockett's *The Help* to see how a southern voice is handled for both black and white races. If you want to throw this bestseller at me as proof that I'm wrong, fine. But remember. Ms. Stockett came from the South. She worked in New York publishing and could get away with more than you can, because, besides being a wonderful writer, she had contacts. If you have the contacts, don't listen to me. (Rather, share your contacts.)

Don't borrow speech patterns from television. If your characters talk *pretty-pretty good*, like the lead character on *Curb Your Enthusiasm*, every editor and agent in America will recognize your lack of originality in stealing from Larry David. Even on a show like *The Closer* (which is not the same as the term we use in this book) Brenda Johnson's verbal tics really did get annoying (even to other characters on the show), and the writers dialed them back in later seasons. Above all, pet phrases that get into the mainstream from pop culture are usually short-lived. Why date your book with trendy wordage?

Don't overuse any tag. In one of my novels, I found a major character using *acourse* (for of course) every other line. Such a device begins to stink after the first hundred or so uses.

Don't strain over creating distinctive speech. If you press too hard, it will show in obvious, repetitive expressions. Your skill at speech tags will improve as you exercise it. Your best efforts will be subtle, graceful, even understated. And they will make for your most memorable characters.

RELEVANT BACKSTORY. This is an important starting place because by knowing the *what* of your story, you will be able to determine a *why* for your character's goals, motivations, and even his fatal flaw. Remember to include only the most important parts of the backstory: What happened before your novel opened to put your master character in conflict with his family. As with the "Pertinent Bio," you'll be able to weave these details into the story later as events unfold and you reveal the past. And you can write details into the backstory as that character develops and reveals new things about his past, things that you had not thought about before, things that will likely come into play deeper into the story.

Caution: Do not open your tale with backstory. Minimize backstory. Stay in the now as much as you can. (Tip of the hat to Donald Maass, author of *Writing the Breakout Novel.*)

GOAL/MOTIVATION. Here you record the most critical goals and urgent motivations of your heroic character. A goal is something that a character feels she *must* to achieve: wealth, love, honor. A motivation is a reason for wanting that goal—greed, love, duty, ambition, and so on. I try to round out a character by enumerating three types of goals in this space.

1. *Career or idealistic personal goals.* The things a character seeks to fulfill a higher call.
2. *Selfish goals.* Everybody has self-interests and base instincts.
3. *Romantic or sexual goals.* This area refers to both the animal urges and love interests of characters.

However you handle goals and motivations, start by asking: What does my character stand for? What does he want? What is he against? Why?

A heroic character's goals and motivations cannot lead to trivial pursuits. Master characters must be given to furious passions, driving forces, lifetime ambitions, and basic values. A character must be willing to risk all, even life, for such things.

Earlier I talked about the universe of the heroic character clashing with the universe of her adversary. Here is where you clarify and document that collision. Whatever the heroic character is for, the heroic character's adversary is against. What the heroine wants, the antiheroine tries to steal.

The central conflict in a novel arises from the powerful, usually violent, struggle between the opposing goals and motivations of the heroic character and his adversary.

You ought to be able to indicate the goals and motivations of each of your master characters by now. So do so.

FATAL FLAW AND SAVING GRACE. When you first tested your novel idea against reality, you read about these concepts (see page 35).

Even the most heroic hero is flawed, often seriously, and the nastiest villain has some saving grace, no matter how small. Here are two reasons why.

1. **Realism.** Flawed heroes and villains with at least one redemptive quality seem more realistic, more human.

2. **Dramatic tension.** You should increase tension in any instance when the heroic character is at risk of being defeated unless she overcomes her flaws. Same for a villain who cannot overcome his saving grace. These are the makings of a real tragedy.

And so on.

Even minor characters should have goals and motivations. Permit them to have personal reasons for being in your novel, rather than using them as set pieces for your convenience.

I warn you, if you don't give this notion of purposeful characters some high-quality thought, you'll end up with boring characters or find yourself resorting to stereotypes: the crotchety cop with a heart of mush, the sleazy playboy always getting his face slapped, and the like.

Connect goals and motivations of major characters to those of the master characters. In life, people play by looser rules than in novels. They don't have to clash or cooperate with each other and often don't care to. In novels, you must establish relationships, causes, and effects. Things happen for reasons, and almost always because of either cooperative efforts or conflicts of interest. So, however tenuously you choose to execute this concept, make it all connect. There's a logic here that increases reader participation. Because readers want to know things that characters don't know and see things that make sense, if only they could arrange them the same way in their own minds.

You might expect the goals and motivations of a major character to coincide with the heroic character's because they're friends. Instead, they clash, making for a better story.

SKETCH YOUR MINOR CHARACTERS

At this stage of your novel, chances are you haven't even met your minor characters. These are the extras, the walk-ons who drop in, drop out, and often never reappear. In a murder mystery, they're the nameless handful of victims who, by their timely deaths, establish that a serial killer is on the loose. Eventually, master and major characters will hurl their courageous selves into harm's way, but in this genre, a few of the little people have to die first.

They're also the surly cabdrivers, tough-talking hookers, pesky little sisters, snotty (or efficient) secretaries, and occasional friends of other characters. When the credits roll at the end of a movie, they're the "Cop #1" and "Fat man in polka-dot pants."

Or maybe they're the original minor characters you create on your own instead of falling back on types.

You can fill in the various blanks these characters in any order you please. Feel free to be brief. You might identify a character as "menacing drunk" in place of a name. You might limit the physical description to only one feature, which might not be striking, as I have defined it here. The distinctive speech might be quite ordinary. Still …

Don't give short shrift to minor characters. Yes, they are minor. But do not blow off a chance to create great characters down to the least walk-on in your book. If you want to examine the work of a master of this concept, read *Lonesome Dove*, by Larry McMurtry, the screenplay for *Shakespeare in Love*, or anything by Mark Twain. Every soul who appeared in those works, even if only for a sentence, seemed remarkable. Take a second look at any novel whose characters swept you away. If you think about it, these were not characters in the story but people, little people as well as the large people, you came to know and love. Or hate.

CHOOSE A POINT OF VIEW

Decide whose voice will be telling the story and whose minds will be open to the reader. In this book, for instance, you know who's talking to you—a dogmatic, bossy writing coach. As such, I'm going to make this decision easy for you by saying:

Use a third-person, past-tense point of view (POV), and limit the novel's omniscience to your master characters.

A brief English 101 refresher is in order. First person is the *I, we, us* narrator. I've used it a lot in this book—in this sentence, in fact. In first-person narration, one character tells the story as she sees it: The reader can know only what goes on in that character's mind and can only guess (along with the I narrator) what's going on in other characters' minds. The action on stage can occur only when the *I* narrator is present. Unless you're a published writer already, don't use first-person narration. Save it for your second or third novel.

This book uses second person even more than first person: "You know what I'm saying, right? Get it?"

Both those questions are forms of second person; the *you* is either stated or implied in the form of addressing the reader. I'm not going to go into detail. Don't even think about using second-person narration in your first novel.

A third-person point of view involves a storyteller, often the detached voice of the author, who tells what happened, usually as it happens. The third-person narrator constructs sentences like this:

Janice Clement flung the door open to a grizzled codger, greasy of face, maybe 70 years old.

"Oh," she said, "sorry. I thought some kids were ringing the bell and running away."

The guy blinked at her. "Hello, Mother," he said, licking a spot of foam from one corner of his drooping mouth.

"What did you say?"

"Hello. Mother."

She slammed and locked the door and went to the phone. Dementia? Probably. She tapped the receiver against her forehead: Cops or the EMTs? The door chimes went off, fast and hard like Morse code. A fist—or was it a foot?—pounded the door. He was shrieking at her. *Mother* had become a four-syllable word.

Cops. Definitely cops.

Notice the point of view. The narrator telling you what Janice sees and thinks—in Janice's voice. She even doubts herself. *Dementia? Probably.*

The storyteller tells using *he, she, they, them, it* terms: "*Janice* flung"; "*He* said"; "*She* slammed."

This is the third-person point of view. Plus, it's in past tense. These are actions and thoughts told as if they have already happened: "Janice *flung*"; "He *blinked*"; "She *slammed*"; "He *shrieked*." Even so, a sense of immediacy is not sacrificed in the telling. Especially when certain dramatic constructions are used, as in "She tapped the receiver against her forehead" and the rest of the passage. You can see the images and feel a tension, right? That's immediacy. What's more, you get a sense of omniscience.

Speaking of which …

The narrator's (storyteller's) limited omniscience. You know what Janice has imagined in the past, you learn that she knows something about dementia, you see her suppressing rudeness, and you can read her thoughts, in italics, as she wrestles with a decision. Going into thoughts and motives is omniscience—a power reserved for gods and writers like yourself.

Yet it's a limited power in this example. Going into the codger's head to get to his thoughts and motives might well diminish this scene by spoiling its mystery.

The idea of limited omniscience—not going into the head of every character—doesn't prevent you, the storyteller, from visiting scene locations where none of the master characters are present. You can write a powerful action scene, entire battles, if you want. You just wouldn't be eavesdropping on the thoughts of all the characters, only relaying their words and chronicling their actions. This is an instance where reader participation comes into play again. Don't try to tell the reader everything from the heads of every character. Let them figure some things out for themselves. In fact, it's often better to fake out the reader. You'll remember the movie, *The Sixth Sense*, with Bruce Willis. And the novel by William Diehl and film *Primal Fear*, starring Richard Gere and Edward Norton and a dozen other great actors. Those demonstrated their impressive ability to fake out readers.

I grant you, telling you to use third-person limited omniscience demands a lot without justifying much. I can't stop you from using a mix of first and third person, present tense, or unlimited omniscience. Some of the best and biggest best-sellers, are done in first-person, some in first person present tense. You and I both have read and enjoyed these stories by award-winning, best-selling authors.

I happen to like first person when the character's voice teems with power and music, the second T in my PARTICIPATIONS?" acronym. If you have such power and music in you, be my guest. Here's a quick rundown.

First Person

The storyteller uses *I, we, me, my, our,* and *us.*

Part of that Janice example if I write it in the first-person present tense:

> I fling the door open to a grizzled codger old enough to be my granddad, 70, maybe 80. Phyllis Diller, only not as pretty.

Advantages of This Point of View

- It feels natural to most writers because we live in an *I*-world.
- You have to deal with only one mind, the narrator's.
- You can create a distinctive internal voice.
- You can add an element of craft telling a story that's not entirely reliable because the storyteller is flawed.

Disadvantages of This Point of View

- You can write only about what the narrator can see or sense.
- The narrator must always be onstage or observing the stage.
- You can't go into the mind of other characters, although *The Help* has a neat twist on first person, just to prove that you can break any rule if you're good enough. Three first-person narrators share the storytelling in *The Help.* Frankly, I liked it. My advice …
- If you write beautiful music in your prose, this is a great POV. If you're merely mortal or less, stick to the third person.

All I can say is, more than anything else you want to write and sell your novel. Your best chance is to show that you can write a decent story, no matter your point of view or tense. Tricky stuff, unless you are a true latent genius, won't help you as much with a first reader in an agent's office or an intern for an editor as much as simply telling a wonderful story simply.

Whether you take my advice or not, you're ready to rumble on your novel.

And this is where you begin, with the best tool yet of any tool I have shown you, the one that will help you tell and sell your story. I'm talking about an acid test of writing, although you may find I spell it oddly.

STEP 5. Get Down to Some Serious Writing

Developing your first two sketches into full-blown incidents using the ACIIDSS test as a writing guide—finding your voice and dialing up its timbre.

Here's what you're going to do in chapter 5:

* Use the Incident checklist as the basis for writing your plot or story structure.
* Rewrite your first draft Incidents using the YCWAN system, especially ... The ACIIDSS Test.
* Evaluate the Opener of a best-seller.
* Avoid mistakes of amateurs.

THE INCIDENT CHECKLIST, A DIGITAL EVOLUTION

When I called them *scenes*, I kept track of them on 5" × 8" (13cm × 20cm) scene cards just as with characters. If I needed to move a scene in my novel, all I did was shuffle the card off to another spot in the deck. I wrote each subplot on cards of a distinct color, then inserted them into the proper place in the main story line. Now you can do all those things digitally, which is better and faster, because you'll be looking at chapter and Incident titles only in Outline View, just as you did with character names, expanding or collapsing each one as you go. All the details stay out of sight until you want to access them with a click of the mouse. You can use a different font color for each subplot. And you can drag an Incident from one spot to another in the story line.

As before, you can download this file, *YCWAN_incident_checklist* from my website, www.writefromparadise.com

Except for the titles, or headlines, of each of these three templates, they're all the same once you expand and use the Outline View in Microsoft Word.

✚ Master, Major, or Minor Incident—in Headlines Only

✚ Opener Incident—in Headlines Only

✚ Closer Incident—in Headlines Only

Now that you have your Opener and Closer sketched out in your own words, style, and logic, you know where your story is going, beginning to end. Let's adapt each of those Incidents to my logic, the Incident checklist.

THE OPENER

Let's work on the Opener, our first Incident, one that you have in draft, or at least in sketch form already.

After you expand a headline by double-clicking on the plus sign, this is roughly what the Opener Incident template looks like. I've added indents for clarity on the page here.

✚ Opener Incident—in headlines Only
Tell what happens in this incident—briefly outline the **ACIIDSS element** you plan to write into each of these segments of the Incident:

In the Beginning of the segment
    Action
    Conflict
    Imagery
    Irony
    Dialogue
    Stories
    Surprise

In the Middle
    Action

Conflict
Imagery
Irony
Dialogue
Stories
Surprise

At the end
   Action
   Conflict
   Imagery
   Irony
   Dialogue
   Stories
   Surprise

Who is in this Incident? Circle the character who causes this Incident.
   Hero?
   Heroine?
   Villain?
   Lover?
   List any others:

Where is the Incident set?
What's the purpose of the Incident?
   Move the story line ahead?
   Introduce or develop characters?
   Introduce or worsen a problem?
   Solve a problem?
   Set up later Incidents?
   Create atmosphere?

What Incident must come before this one?
What Incidents must follow this one?
What is the dominant physical effect in this Incident?
   Sight?
   Sound?
   Taste?
   Touch?
   Smell?
   Light?

Before you start writing your own first Incident, follow along as I demo the Opener from the novel, *Q&A*, the basis for the film, *Slumdog Millionaire*.

To begin with, I retitle the heading: From:+ Opener Incident—in headlines Only; To:+ Opener (prologue)—Jamal jailed for winning millions on a quiz show

Just for the record, the hero in the novel has a different name from the hero, Jamal, in the film, but let's not get into that. It's too confusing, because in the book he has three distinct names with three different purposes. It's a nifty touch, but I'm going to let you decide why this is so on your own if you both see the film and read the novel.

I will leave in the word, Opener, to remind myself that this is one of my most crucial Incidents. Novelist Vikas Swarup made this chapter a prologue. I would have given it a chapter title or number.

I use black type for all Incident headlines of the main story line, all of which involve the hero, if only indirectly. As I said, subplots will appear in a font of the different color so I can tell the main plotline from subplots at a glance.

As for the content of the headline, you won't need anything tricky. You already know it's your Opener. Besides, as if you would forget, I told you to leave the word Opener, right there in the headline. Later, you'll write headlines that act as memory aids to the content of each Incident. That's so you can collapse your entire story line in Outline View and navigate more quickly to the Incident you want to work on next. No more turning pages. No more flipping through cards.

THE ACIIDSS TEST

By now you've figured out that ACIIDSS on the Incident checklist stands for *Action, Conflict, Imagery, Irony, Dialogue, Stories,* and *Surprise.* At a closer look, you'll see that these are also seven elements of the PARTICIPATIONS?" acronym, where *Stories* stands for *Tales.* These seven are your building blocks for writing an Incident. You'll find it useful to look at every Incident, no matter its importance, in three parts. Each Incident is a smaller story within a novel, and each has a beginning, a middle, and an end. And here's where you begin to consider what kind of action will take place in the beginning of this Incident. The middle. The end. Think of them as three acts, if you like.

Let's use the ACIIDSS Test to analyze the beginning segment of *Slumdog Millionaire*'s Opener Incident.

I have been arrested. For winning a quiz show.

That's the opening line of the novel by Vikas Swarup. Nine words.

Conflict, irony, dialogue, and surprise. The irony is huge, and that's why I used it to write my Incident headline. The conflict is obvious. The dialogue is the first-person narrator, the hero of the story, speaking to you. He suggests he will tell you two stories, one about his arrest, the other about winning the quiz show. As you know from seeing the film or reading the novel, that's the basis for the plot, connected at every turn, coming together in the crashing climactic moment of the Closer.

What about dialogue? Why, that's the conversation between the reader and the first-person narrator, whom we're calling Jamal. He's talking to you. You hear him, and you connect at once. Wow! Tell me more, Jamal.

So, what comes next?

> They came for me late last night, when even the stray dogs had gone off to sleep. They broke open my door, handcuffed me, and marched me off to the waiting jeep with a flashing red light.
>
> There was no hue and cry. Not one resident stirred from his hut. Only the old owl on the tamarind tree hooted at my arrest.

We are now seventy-one words into the story, and, I think we have just read the beginning segment of the opening Incident in full.

And what do we see? Action. More conflict—breaking down the door, handcuffing, marching him to the Jeep. And the irony of no fuss in the neighborhood, the sleeping dog lying. The image of that old owl. The sound of the owl. The image of the flashing red light. It haunts me right from the start. The stray dogs flopped in the shadows of the alley, too tired to awaken at the ruckus, create both an image and a tiny tale. In the second sentence, Jamal gives you two stories about breaking down doors and getting cuffed. He lets you supply the imagery and details on your own. Then there is the story of getting marched to a waiting Jeep. You supply the officer at each elbow, and he supplies the flashing red light. The Jeep most likely, still idling.

The middle of the Opener begins with background and some exposition. Well-written because it is so simply written. We get to see a bit of a cynical attitude of the narrator and we learn about the class system and the slums where our hero came from. And as the middle of the Incident comes to its finish, we learn that word had seeped out that he wants something. His fellow waiters threw a party for him after his big win. The middle of the Incident ends with:

The doddery bartender offered me his daughter in marriage. Even the grouchy manager smiled indulgently at me and finally gave me my back wages. He didn't call me a worthless bastard that night. Or a rabid dog.

I think you can fill in the elements here in these three sentences. Action, conflict, irony, imagery, and more stories. He continues his dialogue not only with you but in indirect quotes, from the backstory: In the past the manager had called Jamal a worthless bastard and a rabid dog.

Our hero segues immediately into ...

> Now Godbole calls me that, and worse. I sit cross-legged in a 10-by six-foot cell with a rusty metal door and a small square window with the grill through which a shaft of dusty light streams into the room. The lockup is hot and humid. Flies buzz around the mushy remains of an overripe mango lying squished on the stone floor. A sad-looking cockroach lumbers up to my leg. I am beginning to feel hungry. My stomach growls.

I think you can analyze this well enough on your own. Before reading my opinion, evaluate that paragraph using the ACIIDSS Test.

Let's compare notes, shall we? The irony here is crackling. This kid has an appetite in the midst of squalor. Count the little stories full of action (the sad, lumbering cockroach). Every paragraph has one or more instances of conflict. And we see surprise after surprise, tiny ones to be sure, but every one a delight. Until ...

The Opener Incident begins to pick up its intensity in every aspect of the ACIIDSS Test and for twelve pages you get intense violence in each of the elements of the ACIIDSS Test. As Inspector Godbole begins to torture Jamal.

This middle segment is clearly the meat of the Opener. As the segment unfolds, you learn more about the quiz show. You begin to wonder yourself: *How does the kid rise from the slums with the smarts to win a game show in India like the one you're familiar with in America,* Who Wants to Be a Millionaire? And now that he is a millionaire, if this is the treatment he's going to get, the question takes on a whole new, ironic meaning.

The violence of the torture escalates. The images become more graphic. The dialogue swings from racist and hateful to soft and cajoling. Then, after it lets up, the kid continues to insist that he won the quiz show fairly. Only to bring on even more graphic and violent forms of torture. They give him a confession to sign. All he has to say is that he cheated, and they will stop the torture.

When he refuses the torture gets even worse, always worse. It begins to make you, the reader, dizzy as well. Participation.

Jamal knows he will sign a confession:

After ten, maybe fifteen, more slaps. After five, perhaps six, more shocks.

You believe him. Participation. He won the quiz show fairly—and you don't know how, but already you know it, just know it. Participation. You think he should sign the confession to save his own life. *Sign it. Jamal, it's only money.* (Or maybe you think he should hold out—*It's millions, Jamal. Don't sign; we'll split it if you get out alive. I'll be there for you, man.*) Either way ... participation.

Because you're in the conversation now.

The middle of the Incident segues, using a surprise. A knock at the door and a lovely young woman enters the horrible setting. She's a lawyer. She insists that she is Jamal's lawyer. He is as surprised as the cop, as are you, the reader. The cops back off, and she talks with her client alone. The rest of the Opener is mainly conversation between Jamal and his new and mysterious lawyer, setting up the rest of the book. Less action, little conflict, less imagery. The irony hangs in the air. Literal dialogue carries most of the Incident as Jamal begins to explain how he won the quiz show. He continues to insist that he did not cheat.

She insists that he will have to persuade her. She wants him to tell his story "From question number one" of the quiz show.

And there you have it, the Opener. If you were to diagram this beginning, middle, and end using the letters BME as we used the letters ADZ before, it would look like this:

$$_B\mathbf{M}_E$$

Modest beginning, big middle, medium-size ending. Which is to tell you once again by showing, that just as stories have a dramatic structure, so do Incidents. They might open with high action, conflict, and drama, then tail off. Or they might start slow and rise to an abrupt climactic moment. And all the possibilities between.

To twist a line from George Orwell's *Animal Farm* all Incidents are equal, but a few Incidents are more equal than others. Since we're working with the Opener and Closer, this would be a good time for me to point out the special functions of the Opener.

THE OPENER'S UNIQUE MISSIONS

Grab the Reader in the First One Hundred Words–A Checklist

An editor or agent might read a thousand words before deciding to either reject your work or ask for the full manuscript. But you can't afford to waste a single one of the first hundred words because those words will help create your ... **first impression at the bookstore.**

You might not have much to say about your book's title, cover, preview quotes, or the ad copy that pitches your novel, but any potential book buyer who has been moved by those things to pick up your novel will glance at the first paragraph or two to get a taste of your storytelling ability. Those first one hundred words must snag his interest and hold him like a Velcro-captured cotton ball so that the only time he dares relax his grip on your novel will be to lay it on the counter to fish a wallet out of a pocket. Somebody's going to spend money on you. That's the ultimate participation.

To borrow from Tom Peters, "Is it gasp-worthy?" And from Steve Jobs, is it "insanely great?" To prove that gasp-worthy doesn't require you to go over the top, check out this Opener from the best-seller, *The Help*, by Kathryn Stockett:

> Mae Mobley was born on early Sunday morning in August, 1960. A church baby we like to call it. Taking care a white babies, that's what I do, along with all the cooking and cleaning. I done raised seventeen kids in my lifetime. I know how to get them babies to sleep, stop crying, and go in the toilet bowl before they momma's even get out of bed in the morning.
>
> But I ain't never seen a baby yell like Mae Mobley Leefolt. First day I walk in the door, there she be, red-hot and hollering with the colic, fighting that bottle like it's a rotten turnip. Miss Leefolt, she look terrified a her own child. "What am I doing wrong? Why can't I stop it?"
>
> *It?* That was my first hint: something is wrong with this situation.

By the way, that's 138 words, but I wanted to get to the punch line. Now that you have that example under your belt, take a look at this checklist and refer to the sample to test how well Ms. Stockett did:

This critical segment of your Opener must, at a minimum:

* **Set the tone** of the narrative, including vocabulary, attitude, and harmony of language.
* **Establish** a point of view.

* **Preview the mechanics of the story,** including sentence length and density of paragraphs.
* **Sketch** a suggestion of the setting.
* **Hit the reader between the eyes** with an element of *Oh wow!* at some point in those first one hundred words of writing that I call insanely great.

A tall order, but the opening words in *The Help* do their job. And how. Ever seen a red-hot infant hollering? Did you catch the revolting image of a rotten turnip in the baby's face? Did you hear the voice of the first-person narrator, written without tricky dialect? Did you feel a jarring reaction after *she told of* raising seventeen children? Of a mother terrified of her own child? Of a mother calling her infant *it*? A few paragraphs further down it becomes even harder to stop reading, when our narrator reports on the mother...

> ... she skinny. Her legs is so spindly, she look like she done growed em last week.... Even her hair is thin, brown, see-through.

When I went looking for new books to use as examples in this revision, my eye snagged on that last image on the bottom of the first page, *see-through* hair. Imagery done without smoke and mirrors, without extravagant adjectives or breathless exertion. A picture in my head with just those two words connected by a hyphen, connected with my mind's eye. Truly gasp-worthy.

I knew that the choice of narrator would force the author to be creative. I knew Kathryn Stockett was going to deliver lots of material on the reinvention of our writing, yours and mine. I was a participant in that story. Just by reading my rave review here, I suspect you will be, too.

Go to that superb database of what readers want on Amazon and check out what others have said about this book in their reviews. Remember, you're not looking for explanations of the plot or the setting in the civil rights era of the 1960s in the South. You're looking for the many ways that readers tell you that this story, this writer, this novel, those characters, all played a part in their lives. Making them participants. One example:

> "... so good that I kept running late for everything because I couldn't stop reading it."
>
> — H. CHOI, a reader reviewer

Ladies and gentlemen, we have a participant. H. Choi became so involved in the story, it disrupted his daily life. Another example:

"It grabbed me from page one and I couldn't put it down. The characters felt like real people and I wanted to meet them. The author takes her time developing each character and telling their story. She doesn't rush the story, and yet it moves along at a nice pace, never dragging."

—T. FOSTER, a reader reviewer from California

T. Foster reveals our elements of participation as well. Do you see them? Are you getting a bit excited? Of course you are. You want your readers to react this way, too. A writer can profit from the clues in example two. We're going to talk about those clues before we let the door of this chapter hit us in the behind, to borrow an image from *The Help*.

Right now you should check out other novels. Count the first one hundred or so and read them. (If the hundredth word falls in the middle of paragraph, include the entire paragraph in your sample. This gives the writer a fair chance to finish her thought.) You'll quickly get an idea of what works—and what doesn't.

The First One Thousand Words Milestone–Another Checklist

The purpose of these words is to create a lasting first impression on an editor or agent. The word, *compelling*, gets a lot of mileage in lines pulled from critical reviews. But here I mean it quite literally:

Your first one thousand words must compel an editor or agent past the milestone where she would normally reject a manuscript. The deeper you can force a publishing professional to read into your novel, the greater the likelihood she will eventually be invested deeply enough to buy or represent it.

Use this checklist to evaluate your work's crucial first thousand words:

Functions of the First One Thousand Words

- **Introduce the heroic character** and give clear signals about his personality, appearance, flaws, and strengths. In other words, begin to characterize him, a process that will continue throughout the novel. Force your reader to care about this character. A caring reader is a participant.

- **Introduce, or at least allude to, the heroic character's worthy adversary**, villain, antagonist, whatever term you wish to use. Characterize her as well. A reader who's upset with a character is a participant.

- **Present the surpassing conflicts of the story.** You may have several—and you should—but certainly the most important problem or quest should come into play early. To borrow from Donald Maass, whose *Writing the Breakout Novel* how-to and later workbook of the same title, your novel should drip with conflict on every page. Yes, every page. Remember our point from early on: Nobody ever wrote a best-seller, including the Bible, without conflict. Conflict is the most powerful element for engaging readers as participants. Even if they don't want conflict in their daily lives, they can't help watching it. There is a seedy side to conflict. We call it the television reality show. But you don't have to stoop to that in the art of writing conflict. Since this is a checklist, we'll just leave it at that for now and go into detail later.

- **Deliver evidence of the danger,** suspense, or dramatic irony you might have hinted at in the first one hundred words.

- **Remain true to the tone and mechanics** of the first one hundred words.

- **Foreshadow crucial Incidents** to come in the first fifty to one hundred pages, the point-of-no-return incident.

- **Foreshadow the climax** in some way, however mysteriously.

- **Flesh out the setting.**

- **Demonstrate your ability to write** at least one Incident filled with action, conflict, imagery, and dialogue. You might find it artificial for me to suggest using part of your novel like a resume just to prove you can write certain things. Not at all. If your first one thousand words simply uses narration and exposition, explained the background, described people or settings, and philosophized about action that will come in later chapters, you haven't a prayer of escaping the inevitable rejection pile.

- **Establish a clear central story line** so the reader knows, or thinks she knows, where the story will go.

- No matter how serious your drama, **elicit a couple smiles** and at least one hearty laugh from your readership.

- **Create the taste for** *Oh wow!* at intervals. In my opinion you must satisfy that taste at least once every two thousand words or so for the entirety of your novel. You get an *Oh wow!* and you've nailed participation.

The Opener must deliver proof of an ability to write Incidents filled with precise words and ideas, riveting action, palm-sweating conflict, dazzling imagery, and magical dialogue.

Done properly, such an Incident would accomplish all the other objectives, including making the editor or agent believe your project could make money. Anybody who thinks he can make money with your novel is going to participate. Nuff said?

I can't give you the entire thousand-word opener for *The Help*, but I can give you a taste of where the book is going with only a few samples. Talking about the mother of the newborn again, the novel's first narrator, Aibileen, says …

> Fact, her whole body be so full a sharp knobs and corners, it's no wonder she can't soothe that baby. Babies like fat. Like to bury they face up in you armpit and go to sleep. They like big fat legs too. That I know.
>
> By the time she a year old, Mae Mobley following me around everywhere I go. Five o'clock would come round and she'd be hanging on my Dr. Scholl shoe, dragging over the floor, crying like I weren't never coming back. Miss Leefolt, she'd narrow up her eyes at me like I done something wrong …
>
> I think it bother Miss Leefolt, but Mae Mobley my special baby.
>
> I lost my own boy, Treelore, right before I started waiting on Miss Leefolt….
>
> That was the day my whole world went black. Air look black, sun look black. I laid up in bed and stared at the black walls a my house. Minny came ever day to make sure I was still breathing, feed me food to keep me living. Took three months fore I even look out the window, see if the world still there. I was surprised to see the world didn't stop just cause my boy did.

I don't know about you, but I'm in for the rest of the ride. Aibileen, I want to hear the rest of your story. I want to know how it works out between you and the child, you and the mother. Can I come over and visit? Hear your story?

DEVELOPING YOUR OWN STYLE WITH THE ACIIDSS TEST

Let's use seven elements of the ACIIDSS Test to make you a better writer. I told you to think about what action goes into the beginning, middle, and end of an Incident. Then weigh the conflict in each part of an Incident. And so on.

What do you do first? Let's begin with the easy stuff.

When I say go, start with the tiny sketch you wrote back in chapter 2, plug the details from that sketch into the Incident checklist for your Opener. Copy and paste. Copy and paste. If you have a slice of action sketched out, decide whether it goes into the beginning, middle, or end of the Incident and put it there.

Next, you might have yellow tablets filled with notes. You might have a completed first chapter or Incident that you've taken out of the closet or pulled from under your bed. Note cards, napkins, scraps of paper, whatever.

Just go through your material and take your writing genius out of your system and put it into mine. Have faith. This will work, I assure you. Done? Great. Let's apply some order and substance.

Then insert your cursor and begin writing anywhere in the template that works for you. Answer whatever questions that you can.

You might have a punch line that has been rattling around your head for weeks. Say it goes as a line of your hero's dialogue near the End of the Incident. Insert your cursor after the Dialogue element in the "At the End" segment of the Incident and write the punch line.

Have you already written a great first line? Write that into the "At the Beginning" segment.

But what if you've already written an entire first chapter? How do you convert it to my system?

Maybe you don't need to. Use the ACIIDSS Test checklist as a guide to analyze your Opener. Then see how it stacks up against the unique mission of the Opener, the first one hundred words and so on. If you find that you already have a solid three-act structure to the Incident and each of those segments is packed with the seven elements of the ACIIDSS Test, I see no point in taking your work apart.

Even if you find it lacking in some areas, very likely you can pump up the weaker elements with some of the ideas from this chapter.

No matter where you are, you should study how to develop or improve your style. Style sets you apart from all other writers. Your style is how you talk to readers. It's one of your most powerful tools for getting them to participate in your story.

How to Develop Your Style

What is style? Why, it's you, of course. Style is how you come across to readers in your writing. You are distinctive in a thousand different ways, from your fingerprints to your hair growth (or loss) patterns, your speech, your eating habits, your sense of humor, and your inimitable take on the world. You establish a personal style only by writing.

Malcolm Gladwell, in *Outliers,* talks about success in terms of putting in ten thousand hours of practice. I think that somewhere between the point where you write a half-million words and a full million words, you should be selling your work. That's because you cannot help but develop a sense of grace, scope, depth, and so many other qualities of the best-selling writers if you continue to write and write. In fact, even published writers are like the amateur. They want to get to the next level. They want to break out and achieve a new kind of success because once they have sold a book, they must sell a second. And then a third. And so on. Then comes the realization that they must sell something big.

Take heart. You can get to another level if you keep at it. Writing. All the time writing. Novelist Dean Koontz has hope for all of us: "*Not all popular novelists are good, but all good novelists are, sooner or later, popular.*"

Good novelists work at it. Gladwell says, "… the people at the top don't just work harder or even much harder than everyone else. They work much, *much* harder." To that I would add, they work much, much smarter, using tools like this system. So do you have to write and throw away a million words before you can sell a novel?

No way. I've already pointed out that you don't even have to be a good writer to be a best-seller. And I have a few shortcuts for you. Seven of the elements of PARTICIPATIONS?"

1. Write well-paced *action*.
2. Capitalize on sweaty-palm *conflict*.
3. Create powerful *imagery*.
4. Build some smiles into your story, *irony*, wit, and humor.
5. Start talking to readers with sparkling *dialogue*, if not between characters then between you and readers.
6. Tell tales within your overall novel and within Incidents.
7. Surprise me. Make me gasp with your insane greatness.

Action. Conflict. Imagery. Irony. Dialogue. Story. Surprise. Nothing in there about poetry or lyrical prose.

Action, conflict, dialogue, and story have greater weight in making an Incident work. And, I argue, when you can, write an Incident using each of them. The three remaining elements: Imagery, irony, and surprise are as important as the first four. But if you wrote an Incident absent of one or all of these elements, it would be just fine with your reader. But to consider each of them as you plan an Incident.

Now let's study each element and try to define a scale or continuum. Best of all, let me show you how to use them in writing your first draft. If you must err in this process, err on the side of excess, then tone it down in the editing and revision process.

A few minutes after I wrote the words, *err on the side of excess*, I passed my cursor over a place in the first draft where my editor at Writer's Digest, Melissa Hill, marked up the digital file. Her comment? *This seems a little over the top.* Apparently she'd not known that my middle initials are O.T.T.

I do tend to be excessive to a fault. Which is why I love my wife, editors, and agent, who each in their own way force me to dial it down for public consumption.

Still, I say push the envelope in the early draft. Just make sure you amp down before going final.

Write Well-Paced Action

Novels must move on every page, in every scene, in all your sentences, and if it's not too much to ask, they must move forward to your climactic Closer. This principle applies to every category of fiction from romance to mystery to epic to Western. The best writers sweep you up in the current of a moving story and pull you along like a relentless river. This rule applies to every Incident you write as well. Even narrative passages should create a sense of motion.

Build action into every scene, every passage of dialogue, paragraph, every sentence of your novel. When in doubt, use action.

By action I don't mean fistfights and violence. Characters need not run around shrieking. Think of it as filming a motion picture with your words rather than painting a still life in oils. Action doesn't even require people to move. Sometimes in film, the camera moves while the actors and landscape remain motionless. Sometimes a man is most compelling when he sits remembering, tears welling in his eyes. *Tears welling.* That's the action I'm talking about. *He cried?* Not so much.

Use Active Voice

Using active voice in all your master Incidents increases the pace. A quick grammar primer: When the subject of a sentence performs the action, that is active voice.

Rhonda ate the spider.

Rhonda is the subject of the sentence, the eater; and *ate* is the verb, or action, word. In contrast, when the subject of a sentence is the receiver of the action, that is passive voice.

The spider was eaten by Rhonda.

As before, *Rhonda* is the eat*er*, but she is no longer the subject of the sentence. That's reserved to the eat*ee*, the spider.

Quick grammar quiz. Active or passive voice?

The spider ate Rhonda.

If you chose active voice, congratulations. Active voice uses fewer words than passive. It imparts a sense of immediacy. It identifies the actor performing the action.

By no means am I suggesting you can't use passive voice. Just as the active voice elevates action, the passive mellows an Incident or sets up action to come. Check out this example.

Lamar was overcome by the sheer bleakness of the room, by the gray walls, the flat, green light, the warped windows. As if he were standing inside his own soul looking out.

Here's how I might have begun in the active voice:

Lamar's stomach sank at the sheer bleakness of the room, its gray walls…

This is not about a right answer or a wrong answer on the active voice. It's my way of making you aware of active versus passive. If you are writing entire novels in the passive voice, you are making them, not mellow, but narcotic. This is a tool to jack up the pace or dial down the intensity in an Incident.

It's also used to set up action:

He was hit with a rush of sensations, quick pulse, hot skin, trembling muscles. His body was being mobilized. By rage. Not again. Don't let this happen to me again.

Use Action Words

We're talking about using:

- concrete nouns
- action verbs
- precise adjectives—but sparingly

- rare adverbs—those that cannot be eliminated
- no weasel words like *nearly, almost,* and ones that end in *-ish.*

Of the two selections below, which conveys more action?

> She was so hungry she proceeded to eat very quickly and topped it off with a couple cold ones, Coors—the only beer she'd imbibe. When she had polished off the greasy, unhealthy meal of pork, she almost felt she would burst. In point of fact, she did become ill. She blew chunks, almost getting it all over herself.

Or, using the same number of words:

> She wolfed a baked potato in three bites—no chewing—and gnawed four chops to the bone, fat and all. All grunts and slurps, she chugged one Coors, then another. As she crushed the second can in her greasy fist, she doubled over in full-body spasms. The meal splattered in a pool of chunks between her bare feet.

A brief dissection of the material should serve as a spotlight to the issues involved in creating action.

> She was so hungry ...

This is the writer telling you something about the character. Adding the adverb *so,* emphasizing the point, is too lame to debate. The action in the second selection shows you just how hungry the woman is, using verbs like *wolfed, gnawed,* and *chugged.* Implied action and clear images grow out of words formed from words such as *baked, bites, chewing, grunts,* and *slurps.*

> ... she proceeded to ...

An utter abomination. Never use this construction. Not only is it a waste of words that take up space between a subject and a verb, it also shows a tendency of the author to sound pedantic.

> ... eat very quickly ...

Don't use *very* this way. *Very* points the finger at a writer straining to heighten intensity, a writer too lazy to look up a precise verb. That leaves *eat quickly.* Why not *gobble, scarf, bolt,* or *wolf*?

> ... topped it off with a couple cold ones ... polished off ...

Not so terrible but too informal—unless the narrator is consistently informal—and imprecise besides.

... the only beer she'd imbibe ...

Imbibe? Come on.

... greasy, unhealthy meal of pork ...

The author is telling you he's the health nut, more so than the character. Anyhow, it's never a good idea even for characters to preach, either to other characters or to the reader. And another thing, the author is telling the reader again rather than showing. Who doesn't know pork is greasy? Contrast it with the same adjective in the second selection. A *greasy fist* is the result of eating with your fingers—the words create an image, not a narrative declaration.

In point of fact ...

Office language.

... she did become ill ...

Such an innocent phrase replete with sins: vague, redundant to *blew chunks*, and euphemistic. Contrast that to the image of bare feet straddling the mess. Makes me queasy seeing and hearing it spatter. I can feel, well, never mind.

... She blew chunks ...

Better than the previous segment because it creates an image, though it may be a dated phrase.

... almost getting it all over herself.

Weasel.

Dial Up the Conflict

Use conflict to elevate action. Conflict results when two characters want the same thing. Or when one opposes the other's goal. Or when outside forces become obstacles to your heroic character's achievement of his worthy goal.

Conflict invites full-blown action. Conflict sets the pulse of the reader racing. Conflict keeps a novel moving. Conflict is the one indispensable ingredient in every best-seller.

Conflict might be simply a subsurface tension on one end of the scale with frenetic combat on the other. Between those extremes you might instill simple passive-aggressiveness, leading to open hostility, ascending to injury, ending in fatality.

Never set the throttle of your novel to cruise on placid seas. If you're not incorporating a full-blown typhoon, you ought to at least be painting an ominous cloud. If you're ever tempted to spend a few pages of your novel reveling under clear skies, don't. Incorporate a suspicious ripple that might mean a great white shark lurking beneath the surface or a tsunami building over the horizon. Otherwise, people will skip those pages. Conflict moves a novel because the reader relishes a battle, even a small one, heck, even an imagined one.

How else do you explain the audience for shock radio, combative political interviews, and TV magazines? What's common to every successful television show, whether a comedy or a drama? Conflict, of course. You think *Seinfeld* would be funny if everybody got along? Nope. The only times the characters on that show cooperated were when they were organizing a conflict with others or racing toward a showdown of their own. It's the conflict, ma'am, the conflict that makes a hit a hit. Without it, you might as well be writing a dictionary.

I won't address the obvious methods of pumping up conflict. If you don't already know that a lovers' spat, a court battle, a car chase, and a shoot-out are examples of overt conflict, you need more help than this book can give you.

More likely you want to advance your skill at building conflict into a static scene. Let's try it.

Here's some raw material from my novel *Cottage 13*:

> A bare, gray classroom, 15 feet by 30 feet, in the maximum security lockup of a juvenile detention facility. Fluorescent lighting. The west windows look out on a rec yard. The east windows reveal the hallway of a cell block.

What could be more static than an empty room? Let's experiment with ways of creating conflict within it.

Techniques for Incorporating Conflict
Compare a static scene to an active one. Use verbs and verb forms.

> This was a classroom? Add some clanging bars and scowling faces, and it'd be no different than the cellblock across the hall.

Contrast.

> Not exactly the teaching heaven he'd seen in this month's *Modern Educator* magazine. No computers. No projection televisions. No budget. No hope.

Offend the senses.

... stale, dank air—even the light was repugnant, yellow, and warped through the film on the windows.

Establish a point of view. See through the character's eyes.

Outside he could see the rec yard, its fence topped with razor wire. Beyond its coils lay the hills, the sea, freedom. If only he could get them to see that far.

Use a spoken point of view.

"What do you think?" the sergeant asked.
"Stinks."
"Grim all right. Maybe you could work with it. Coat of paint. Couple posters."
"I mean the air. It stinks. Literally."

Make it an issue of dispute.

"I'll spruce it up. Maybe a coat of paint. Something beige or tan."
"Leave it gray," the warden said. "I don't want them forgetting they're in jail. You can't have them start liking it here."

Hitchhike on action.

He pinned the kid against the wall and watched his color change from lifeless gray that matched the paint to strobing blotches of purple.

Plant a seed of mystery or foreshadow a problem.

Lamar vowed to make this class different from the last one. Different paint, different kids, oh yeah, different outcome.

Flash back or visualize.

His last classroom, the one he'd been fired from, had been this barren once. He'd brought in posters, plants, and a piano. He'd brought life to it with pulsating walls and singing children. And a principal who hated his guts.

Create Powerful Imagery

If anyone at all in the publishing business reads your writing sample, the first person to do so likely will be an intern or associate on the first rungs of the business. That means somebody young, probably in her twenties. She's a product of MySpace, Will Ferrell movies, *Sex and the City*, iPods, iPhones, iPads, Blackberries, Facebook, Amazon, Twitter, and YouTube. She starts her day with a nonfat decaf latte and sample chapters from two equally brilliant writers. Yours is full of static description. His sings with action. Even the images at rest create an impression of motion, direction, cause, effect, and consequence. What is going to start this woman's pulse racing? Neither the decaf nor your pages of description.

How do you create images that work? In many ways, some artificial or mechanical, others subtle and artful. Usually, great images burst like fireworks in Incidents featuring gripping action and tense conflict. Here are some tips for creating powerful imagery:

PAINT THE IMAGE IN SMALL BITES. Never stop your story's momentum to write long descriptive passages. Anytime you've written a third consecutive sentence of static imagery, you've crossed a line where your novel risks coming to a halt. One of today's best-selling authors throws on the brakes to stop the story every time she introduces a character. Even walk-ons get a full paragraph or two of description complete with wisecracking observations in the mind of the main character. When you read her books you begin to recognize the parts you can skip without losing your place in the story. That, by definition, is opting out of participation.

INCORPORATE IMAGES INTO ACTION. Good example:

> He saw her duck through the waterfall of glass beads, his bedroom doorway. The beads made the clicking of a rosary.
> She crossed the threadbare rug and looked up into his downcast eyes.

Bad example:

> She came into the room. The rug on his bedroom floor was threadbare. As she crossed it, she stood there, his eyes downcast. He was taller than her.

That's description. Static. The author is talking. Can you hear him? He's describing stuff, and the action sags into the shadows. In the good example, the images are woven into the action of walking and looking. As the character, not the author, sees them.

SALT DIALOGUE WITH NONINTRUSIVE IMAGES.

> She toyed with the fuzz on his ear.
> "Don't," he said, hating the quaver in his voice.
> "You're sweating bullets, little man."
> He slapped droplets off his upper lip. "It's hot."

A quaver in a voice. That's an image. So is toying with somebody's ear, and droplets of sweat on a lip. Quick strokes. **Caution:** Don't overdo this idea of adding an image or action to every spoken line. Too many of those become speed bumps breaking up a fast-paced dialogue.

USE A TINY BUT TELLING DETAIL. Like the harvester ant, the smallest detail can pack a lot of freight. In my last example above, I offer the droplets and his annoyance at them, and his defensiveness.

CHOOSE ACTION-BEARING VERBS.

> She went for his ear again. He slapped her hand away. She stormed out, whipping through the torrent of beads, tramping across the creaking linoleum, careening across the sagging porch and into the sopping night. After he could no longer hear the crunch of her step, one bead string broke. He heard glass beads rolling in the rumples of the kitchen linoleum.
>
> He'd find them tomorrow and re-string them, repair the gap in the waterfall. They'd be on the east side, the low side, where the water pooled every time it rained.

Toyed, stormed, tramped, whipping, careening these words do so much more than say what is. They indicate action, anger, tension, conflict.

CHOOSE ACTION-BEARING NONVERBS. *Clicking* is a verb form used as a noun. *Quaver*, for example, is used as a noun, but it's also a verb in another context. "*Rumples* of *linoleum*," "*sagging porch*," "*sopping night*" all imply action because they are forms of verbs.

CONNECT TO KNOWN IMAGES. Here I'm talking about similes and metaphors without using the grammatical terms. The curtain beads made the clicking of a rosary.

INVENT FRESH SETTINGS. The boy's bedroom has a waterfall of glass beads for a door? Suppose she'd crawled into a pup tent he'd put up in the backyard.

SHOW AN UNUSUAL SIDE OF COMMONPLACE SETTINGS. Place a wall-sized, high-definition projection television screen in this shack and you create a different image.

SHOW AN UNCOMMON USAGE OF COMMON LANGUAGE. The woman didn't exit the shack into the *steamy* night. Too automatic. *Sopping night* suggests the highest possible humidity short of rain. It's also a verb form.

SEE THROUGH THE CHARACTER'S EYES. Hear through his ears. Feel through his skin. Bad example:

> Glass beads rolled in the rumples of the kitchen linoleum.

Good:

> He heard glass beads rolling …

Get it? When you can, use the character's senses instead of the author's.

CREATE AN IMAGE WITHOUT SAYING SO. In our example, it's a shanty where the kid lives. Do you doubt it?

Build Irony Into Your Story

> "I don't read as much as I used to. I read more when I was trying to learn how to write. I read a lot of Hemingway, until I found out he doesn't have much of a sense of humor."
>
> — Elmore Leonard

If you can get the reader to smile, better yet, laugh, she is playing a part in your story. She is reacting emotionally because you either warmed the cockles of her heart or tickled her funny bone.

You can use irony on the level of being funny without resorting to lame humor or smart-aleck quips you hear so often in action movies.

I admit, I'm not the best person to ask about avoiding lame humor. But I like to read writers who don't take themselves too seriously and write their tough guys with a sense of humor.

Elmore Leonard in person must have a terrific, dry wit, judging from the number of characters in his books who are funny without cracking a smile. Lee Child in his novel, *Echo Burning*, puts tough guy Jack Reacher into a hysterical situation without going slapstick. Reacher, trying to pass himself off as a ranch hand, is ordered to saddle a horse, but it's all he can do to figure out which way the saddle goes. Once he does, a young girl has to tell him to start over because he forgot to use a saddle blanket. Reacher is at his funniest when he has to remind himself that horses have hoofs, not feet. *Or is it hooves?* he wonders.

In my army career, I found that men in the most trying, deadly situations can find some kind of dark humor. So even those Bruce Willis wisecracks at the brink of death aren't all that incredible to me.

Your sense of humor will dictate the extent of the irony in your stories. It's not a thing you can spin out of whole cloth—if you try, the effort will show. Even so, I give you three examples to illustrate ways to use irony which, from the overt to the subtle, act like an injection of emotion, pumping life into dialogue. Overt irony:

> "I'm such an idiot," she said.
> "Yes," he said, "You are."

Over the top (hat tip to Ring Lardner):

> "Are we lost, daddy?" I asked.
> "Shut up," he explained.

Subtle:

> I'm such an idiot," she said.
> He did not contradict her.

Elmore Leonard is not above having one character tell a joke to another. Which is, of course, telling the joke to you, the reader. Be wary of that.

Don't struggle over irony, but don't fight it, either. Don't borrow from sitcoms. Take note when a situation brings out a wry smile in you. It's worth trying to capture that smile to share with readers. Get them to smile, and they are literally into your story.

This does not address the larger, literary sense of irony. On a superficial level, it's ironic that in *Slumdog Millionaire* the hero's quiz show questions all relate to slices of his life. It's a supreme tragic irony that Romeo finds Juliet in a drug-induced sleep and, thinking she is dead, takes poison. Whereupon she awakens and finding Romeo dead, stabs herself. A love that cannot be on earth can only find peace in death. Ironic, eh?

In *The Lovely Bones* by Alice Sebold, the narrator of the novel is dead.

If I were to tell you that the name of a character with a cameo in the latest novel I'm trying to market is Saint Judas Iscariot, you would see the irony in that. Wouldn't you? No? Well then, how about Saint Richard Nixon? Ironic enough for you?

You see, irony points to the author's soul, or soul of wit, if you like. You can take yourself too seriously. If you go after every word with a microscope on first draft, you'll see each tree, but you'll never see the forest.

I've found I'm a better writer when I can drink from the cup of irony rather than labor along sipping from the cup of gravity.

Think. Aren't all the best fiction and film laced with irony, both light and heavy? Yes, including *Schindler's List*. If you want to argue, read *Man's Search for Meaning* and argue with Viktor Frankl, please.

Write Killer Dialogue

Dialogue will make or break your novel. Effective dialogue cannot be faked. It works or it doesn't. And it's so easy to check out. An editor or agent can flip to a page in your sample chapters and see and read any dialogue. So all of it has to be good. If the selection she chooses to read is boring, pointless puff, you're busted. No matter what goes on below, let this be your cardinal rule: *Every line of dialogue counts.*

Principles and Pitfalls of Using Dialogue

Dialogue exchanges offer some of the best opportunities for action and conflict. Follow a few simple principles and even the very first scene you write can look professional.

USE DIALOGUE IN ALL YOUR MASTER INCIDENTS. Such Incidents are far too important to leave the inherent action and conflict to a narrator droning on. Let the characters enrich these invaluable Incidents through dramatic exchanges or internal conversation.

WHERE YOU SEE CONFLICT, EXPLOIT IT WITH DIALOGUE. As you hear the narrator in your head describing conflict anywhere on the scale from mere tension to frenetic combat, ask yourself if you can use dialogue to heighten the conflict.

ALWAYS INCORPORATE CONFLICT INTO YOUR DIALOGUE EXCHANGES. If your characters aren't quarreling, at least show them in disagreement—even if it's merely a passive-aggressive attitude on the part of one character and the other isn't aware of it. If a character is alone in an Incident, permit her to carry on a running argument with herself. Your first step in boredom avoidance is: If a line of dialogue doesn't indicate conflict or isn't leading up to conflict, don't bother writing it. Use some other narrative device.

CONSIDER YOUR DIALOGUE ATTRIBUTIONS. Study this brief exchange. Find its flaws and get ready to apply a few new principles.

"I'm concerned about you," she said.

"Why?" he grinned ironically.

"You haven't been yourself lately," she added.

"Whose fault is that?" he smirked.

She continued, "Is it mine, do you think?"

"Yes!" he snorted. "You made me lose Vicky."

"Oh, no," she argued. "You're wrong!"

Did you catch the attributions *added* and *continued*. They're unnecessary synonyms for *said*. I'd expect you also to identify the words *smirked* and *grinned* as body language that cannot be verbalized. If you accept *snorted*, I invite you to try snorting the word *yes*.

But, hey, that's routine stuff. The real problem with this passage? The exchange is flat. The writer missed chances to heighten the conflict and incorporate action, because he didn't adhere to the principles in this chapter.

USE DIALOGUE TO CREATE ACTION. Dialogue exchanges invite action. Here are three ways to capitalize on that.

Show emotion rather than using attributive helpers. Above, the author writes, "she argued." You often see such helpers: "she joked," "he admitted," "she said hotly." Such instances indicate nothing less than a lack of effort. The writer didn't write dialogue that could stand alone so she tried to prop up a line with helping language. If somebody is joking, arguing, admitting, or saying hotly, let the language inside quotes convey that meaning.

CRAFT NONVERBAL LANGUAGE. The man in the example below carries on his side of the conversation twice without saying a word. Once he raises an eyebrow, accepted as an expression of a question. Next he turns his back on her, and you know what that means. Take a look:

"What are you doing here?" he said.

"I'm concerned about you," she said, laying a hand on his shoulder. "I wanna help is all."

"Don't bother." He shrugged off the hand. "I already got a mom."

"All this hostility. Where is it coming from, honey?"

He raised an eyebrow at her.

"Honey."

He turned his back to her.

USE DIALOGUE EXCHANGES TO MOVE THE STORY LINE FORWARD. Don't just create scenes with people talking. Create Incidents within Incidents, like the one above. Introduce problems, enlarge conflict, or solve them in part—that's moving a story line forward.

Caution: I warn you again. Don't tag every line of dialogue with action, behaviors, thoughts, and attributions—let dialogue find its own momentum where characters play off each other's words. This is most important as conflict builds, emotions flare, and the pace quickens in an Incident.

PICK UP THE PACE IN DIALOGUE. Write snappy exchanges. Let your characters use contractions and fragments. Let them bark at each other once in a while, not by saying, *"No," he barked.* Rather, write, *"Hell, no."*

You can't write explanatory patter, slap on quotes, and call it dialogue.

BREAK UP LONG PASSAGES. Use two or three exchanges instead of one long dialogue passage.

ESTABLISH A RHYTHM. The heroine speaks, the villain responds, the heroine shoots back, the villain asks a question, the heroine responds, putting the villain down cruelly.

USE DIALOGUE EXCHANGES TO CHARACTERIZE. If a woman is always dishing dirt on the person she's talking to, you don't have to suggest that she'd talk about your hero when he's out of the room. That's her nature.

LET PUNCTUATION SIGNAL A CHANGE OF SPEAKERS. With two speakers, you won't have to identify each by name or attribute every line of dialogue with *he said/ she said.* A new paragraph does that when it begins with the double quotes.

In lengthy exchanges, have one character use the other's name or use it yourself in attribution, but don't overdo either technique. The distinctive flavor of a character's words should identify the speaker.

By the way, if a speaker should continue one paragraph of dialogue into another without interruption (and I don't recommend it), leave the closing quotes off the end of the first paragraph. Use opening quotes on the second paragraph. Close the second passage of dialogue in the normal way. It's always better for one speaker to react to another. The shorter the speeches, the more you engage the reader in participation. The less you fall into the trap that follows.

AVOID PREACHING, TEACHING, AND SPEECHING. Once upon a time there was the television show *Designing Women.* In every episode, the character Julia Sugarbaker would go off, lecturing the other characters and the audience on some social issue. Shouting, ranting, boring. Her raving sermons became a staple of the show. I can't imagine a better example of what never to do in the dialogue—or narrative, for that matter—of a novel.

AVOID SMALL TALK. Not a single word. Don't begin dialogue exchanges with three lines like this before getting to the meat of your story:

> "Hi, Bob."
>> "Well, hello, Sal. Long time no see. What's happening?"
>> Sal squinted, confused. "Not much. What do you want?"

As a reader, that's what I want to know. Granted, people in our world do talk like that. Not in good fiction, though (although I must confess that in the movie *Pulp Fiction*, I was mesmerized at the effectiveness of double meanings and undercurrents in the film's small talk). Better in your novel to start the same Incident this way:

> Sal planted herself between Bob and the TV set. "You've got thirty seconds," she said. "What's so important that it can't wait till the hockey game's over?"

As in the earlier exchange between the boy and the woman in his bedroom, just assume that all the small talk has already taken place or will never take place. Start your dialogue exchange with a suggestion of conflict. Otherwise, you'll condition the reader to skip the first three or four lines of every passage of dialogue.

Tell Tales Within Each Incident of Your Novel

Easy enough to understand that a novel is a story. Every plot and subplot is a separate story line that ties into the main story. Every Incident is a story in its own right within your novel, the overall story. Tell stories within Incidents to bring every Incident alive.

In the conflict between the young man and woman (see pages 83–85), there is a detail about a broken string of beads, each bead making its own noise on the floor. This is far more than just description. It's even more than imagery. It's action, the result of the conflict, and it's a tiny Incident, told as a story, within the larger Incident.

Remember the opening Incident of *Slumdog Millionaire*? I told you about several stories in the first seventy-one words. Just simple sentences. Even sentence fragments. Remember these tiny stories?

> They broke open my door …

Handcuffed me

… marched me off to the waiting jeep with a flashing red light
Only the old owl on the tamarind tree hooted at my arrest.

You could argue semantics, I suppose. You could say those aren't tales, but action or flashbacks or images or atmosphere. Whatever. I prefer to think of them as tiny tales. Fall into this habit: Tell tiny tales.

Take a look at any best-seller. The main story is filled with large and telling Incidents (chapters, scenes, segments, what have you). Every non-seller is built of the same stuff, tales and detales woven into a coherent, unified larger tale.

What sets the best-seller apart are the tiny tales. Go back and look at the best-sellers, even the badly written ones, modern or classic. *Lonesome Dove, Gone Tomorrow*, anything Twain, *The Odyssey*. You want to be a best-seller or a writer of classics? Write the tiny tales.

I don't know if I'm a typical reader, but I do know that I am a typical magazine editor. It isn't always the big stories that sell me. It's the little ones.

A lady sends me a photograph of two ravens, one squawking into the other's ear. The second bird stares into the camera, a glum look smeared all over his fat beak. The sender wrote, "As if he is saying, 'Enough already.' "

I bought the image.

An artist sends me a watercolor of a paint horse, not to be ironic about it. I use it for the magazine's Christmas card inside the back cover. She writes back to say that she is thrilled because the horse had died of cancer and painting it brought it back to life for her, giving her joy. A story I shared with my readers, of course.

A woman sends me a recipe for homemade limoncello, the recipe itself is maybe fifty words. Her explanation on why to keep it in the freezer and how to serve the Italian liqueur sells me by setting my mouth to watering. I tell you, on a steamy summer night, a shot of this in a glass of lemonade and you will never drink lemonade any other way. And, just to ensure your participation, I posted the recipe on my website, www.writefromparadise.com.

Are you getting my point? It's not just the grand-scale story that sells your novel. It's the tiny tales that propel your novel to the next level. Stories within stories within stories.

Try this yourself. I opened *Slumdog Millionaire* to a random page. On 133, I found these tiny tales:

(My shack) vibrates violently whenever a train passes overhead. There is no running water and no sanitation.

... we live like animals and die like insects. Destitute migrants from all over the country jostle with each other for their own handful of sky in Asia's biggest slum.

There are daily squabbles—over inches of space, over a bucket of water—which at times turn deadly.

(The slum's) open drains teem with mosquitoes. Its stinking, excrement lined communal latrines are full of rats, which make you think less about the smell and more about protecting your backside. Mountains of filthy garbage line on every corner, from which rag pickers still manage to find something useful.

And at times you have to suck in your breath to squeeze through its narrow claustropho- ...

That's where the page breaks. Did you participate by finishing the story in the sentence? See what I mean? Yes, yes, you could argue that much of this crosses over into action, conflict, imagery, and even irony and dialogue. But what's the downside to that? Check out *Slumdog Millionaire*, a novel, on your own. Any Lee Child novel. Any best-seller.

Caution: Don't think of telling tales, the first T in participation, as an academic box to check in your novel's writing checklist. Think of it as the essence of your art. Use every element in your toolbox.

But not randomly. We were speaking of artists earlier. I wrote a magazine story on a woman with hundreds of brushes in cups beside her easel. She can use every brush on every painting. She used every brush she needed to make that painting work.

Use every one of yours to tell tales great and small. Should you ever want to become a best-selling author, you will have to sharpen your telling of the small tales more so than the grand-scale ones. You tell the tiny tales well, and the grand ones will take care of themselves. Take that to the bank. Literally.

Surprise Me

I think you should get into the habit of finding a way to elicit an *Oh wow!* from a reader in every Incident. Could be something as simple as an ironic word choice. Remember way back when in this book when I first used the word, *detales*? Then again just awhile ago? Did you react to it? Love it or hate it, your reaction probably was mild surprise. *Oh, it's not a typo at all. I get it.*

Surprise is a twist at the end of the cliché: *Her reputation white as slush.*

An action that ends in a surprise. You probably saw the Indiana Jones movie where the swordsman showed off his twirling, slashing circus act as he was about to attack. Indiana ended the Incident by pulling a pistol and shooting the guy. End of story for that master swordsman. All that twirling practice gone to waste.

There's that sentence fragment above: "Destitute migrants from all over the country jostle with each other for their own …" Your mind wants to finish the thought: *square meter of dirty earth.* But, no, Swarup writes: "handful of sky." Surprise, people. That, my friends, is participation.

No Hollywood film worthy of the name ends without a surprise, sometimes several. Remember how long it took to kill the stalker in *Fatal Attraction*? *Slumdog Millionaire*, the novel, is full of surprises. Perhaps even more than the movie.

Sure, surprises can lead to the feeling of gimmickry. Don't worry about that in writing your first draft. Just consider it. When in doubt, surprise.

Later, you can always reconsider.

Let me show you some surprises that won't spoil the plot of the novel, *Slumdog Millionaire.*

Jamal reaches his hand through a hole in the wall to comfort the troubled girl who lives on the other side by holding her hand. Salim is amazed because it's

> … the same hole through which rats and cockroaches come into our room.

Jamal reports…

> I don't know how long I hold (the girl's) hand, but when I wake up the next morning I find myself lying on the ground with my hand still thrust through the hole and a family of cockroaches sleeping peacefully inside my shirt pocket.

Surprise.

Jamal scavenges food and tells about how Salim used to eat well by joining marriage processions.

> The bride's side thinks you are from the groom's family and the groom's side thinks you are from the bride's family.
>
> But he gave up the habit after an episode in Nariman Point, when he gate-crashed a marriage where the families of the bride and groom had a massive fight that degenerated into fisticuffs. Salim got beaten up by both parties.

You see, it's not just that he got caught, but that since neither party knew him, they each assumed he was from the other side, so both parties beat him. Now that's an unintended consequence, eh? *Surprise!*

One final example that is a surprise to Jamal, but not to some readers, the devotees of the crossword puzzle who know the answer to this one. Jamal stands looking across the river in Agra, India, gazing at the marvel of a swelling dome with four pointed arches flanked by minarets. He asks a passerby what the building is, and the passerby probably gives the same answer as you, though probably not as kindly.

> "… if you don't know that, what are you doing in Agra? That is the Taj Mahal, idiot."

AVOID BLUNDERS THAT BRAND YOU AN AMATEUR

I have a list I call Ten Bumper Stickers That Cry Out "I'm an Amateur." The list is a compilation of mistakes (not including misspellings and typos) of content and structural errors many beginning writers make. Avoid them and you'll have a step up on all the first-time novelists who don't have this book to coach them along. Paraphrasing Jeff Foxworthy's popular comedy routine, here goes.

You might be an amateur if …

1. YOU WRITE ENDLESS SYNONYMS FOR *SAID*. Perhaps you've seen (or written) lines of dialogue such as these:

> "You're an animal," she said.
> "Am not," he replied.
> "Are too," she countered.
> "Oh yeah?" he challenged.
> "Yes. A pig," she added.
> "Am not," he sneered.
> "Are too," she continued.
> "A pig?" he grinned. "Really?"
> "A *fat* pig," she emphasized.

When you examine any best-seller, I'll wager you never find such instances of dialogue, even in a badly written best-seller. The pro does not write like that. She understands that *said* is an invisible word. If the context does not tell a reader who is speaking, and especially when three or more characters engage in dialogue, *said* does the job without becoming intrusive.

Having said that, let's break the rule. You surely sense by now how little respect I have for rules. It's true, even for my own. So I wrote these lines to amuse myself:

"Damn you," she prayed.

"I'm going to vomit," she spewed.

"Thomas Edison," he invented.

"Can't you see the tears in my eyes?" she cried.

"Such a ghastly, ghostly moon," he waxed.

"Whopper," she ordered, "on the double, and don't you dare put onions on it."

"Stop and think," she blurted.

"I think I am," she philosophized.

"Oh, and two plus two equals five," she added.

"From this moment, I dedicate myself to total silence," she vowed. "And poverty. Oh, and chastity."

"I never interrupt," she interjected.

"Ding-dong," she chimed.

"I dot a code," she sniffed.

"I hear he's a thief and a liar," she slurred.

I hope you'll be amused, too, and perhaps invent some of your own and send them along so I can post them on my Website. You know, participate. But, as a rule, avoid this blunder and the next one in your quotable exchanges.

2. YOUR CHARACTERS SNEER, GRIN, AND LAUGH THEIR WORDS. Avoid constructions that appear in the previous sample dialogue. It makes no more sense to write " 'Am not,' he jogged," than to write "he sneered." If you must indulge in a sneer, write a separate sentence, something like:

"Am not." He sneered at her, inviting a comeback as witty as his own.

3. YOU USE COUNTLESS -LY WORDS. Usually called adverbs, these words rarely carry a story line authoritatively. The amateur author severely taxes her brain, striving earnestly to write professionally, only to find herself crying softly, "One rejection after another." Avoid *-ly* constructions by finding a precise verb that expresses your meaning. Instead of *crying softly*, write *whimpering*. Try eliminating the *-ly* word altogether. In this very paragraph you could strengthen the material by deleting *severely*, *earnestly*, and *softly*, although *usually*, *rarely*, and *professionally* would have to stay to pinpoint the meaning I intended.

4. YOU OVERUSE ADJECTIVES. Piling on adjectives will weaken your writing. Don't use adjectives redundantly. Calling a diamond *white*, *hard*, *sparkling*, and *valuable* adds nothing but words. The meaning is not improved, because the concept of diamond includes all of the above. If the diamond is *black*, *soft*, *dull*, or *worthless*, by all means use those adjectives, which contrast with the accepted notion of a diamond. Unless you mean a lump of coal, in which case, you're back where you began.

Don't use worthless adjectives. James Thurber on the subject of worthless adjectives:

> " 'There's that goddam pretty again,' Ross would say. The easy overuse of *pretty* and *little* exacerbated his uneasy mind. Once, to bedevil him, I used them both in a single sentence—'The building is pretty ugly and a little big for its surroundings.' "

Little, *large*, *pretty*, and even *beautiful* are worthless. They're as lazy and imprecise as the people who use them. Think about it. What is a little stone? Why it's a *pebble*, of course. Littler? Fine. Give it an exact dimension, say, 3 millimeters. That's little enough, unless you find it in your chowder or your kidney.

The final words on adverbs and adjectives: Of course you can use them in your writing, but be precise and deliberate. Always try using verbs and nouns before resorting to adjectives and adverbs. A concrete noun partnered with a precise verb will kick butt on adjectives and adverbs any day of the week.

5. YOU USE THOSE WEASEL WORDS. *About*, *appears*, *approximately*, *probably*, *seems*, *halfway*, and all *-ish* constructions are more examples of weasel words that kill precision. For instance, can you find anything to redeem an expression like "He almost exploded"? Do you mean he seethed? That he stifled his anger? Instead of halfway angry, do you mean annoyed? Irritated? Riled? Be somewhat exact about it, okay? *Precision*, remember. The first word in the PARTICIPATIONS?" acronym.

6. YOU WRITE IN OFFICE LANGUAGE. "At this point in time …"; "in order to effect meaningful change …" Only a bureaucrat writes like that. Don't you. Sure, sure, you may have characters who talk like bureaucrats. Still. Be careful. It's no saving grace to blame a bored reader on a boring character.

7. YOU RELY ON CLICHÉS. This item is obligatory for any writing handbook. Beware the automatic phrase, such as "white as snow" and "quiet as a mouse." If your heroic character roars like a lion, she'd better be a lioness. Write clichés freely into your first draft is what I say. Then, in revision, put a twist or surprise into them. "*How white was it? I'll tell you how white it was. White as hail.*" There. Two twists for good measure.

8. YOU WRITE DIALECT. 'Nuff's arready bin sed on that there isshew.

9. YOU REPEAT YOURSELF OVER AND OVER. Even the pros get stuck on their pet phrases. I'll bet the word *inexorable* appears a dozen times in the late Michael Crichton's *The Lost World*, when no novel ought to use a five-syllable word that calls attention to itself after its first use. Worse yet is to repeat plot information. For instance, a wife's infidelity might appear as a master scene played out in some detail. If she later is struck by guilt and finds she must explain herself to her husband, there's little point in repeating much of anything that the reader already knows. If the husband asks, "What happened?" you might write, "She told him, glossing over the graphic parts." If, when she's finished, the stunned husband asks, "But why?" you can add new information, expanding the plot problem without being redundant. If later yet the husband finds himself explaining to his attorney why to file for divorce, there's no need to repeat anything but the sketchiest of details. Trust the reader not to forget, and move on, please.

10. YOU'RE JUST TOO PRECIOUS. Number ten in the list of amateur mistakes might be the worst—a mortal sin that covers a multitude of venial ones. I doubt anything could cause an editor to reject your manuscript faster than for you to be cute or coy. The following are signs you may be too precious in your manuscript, and I admit, *I'm at risk here every time I pick up a loaded keyboard and start shooting from the fingertips.* Or should I say, *I'm at risk here every time I pick up a loaded digital recorder and start shooting from the lip.*

- Using language and predicaments right out of sitcoms, movies, or even the day's news.

- Being playful with famous names (Jay Letterman and David Leno? Jon O'Brien?).

- Writing annoying gimmicks, such as admittedly awful alliteration—a series of words that begin with the same letter. And add to this the practice of starting every other sentence with *but* or *and*. But also avoid using weird punctuation like multiple exclamation points!! Oh wow! is an exclamation and deserves the mark. You're not very clever!!! is not an exclamation, and, well, you're not very clean if you can't find three verbs and nouns to make your point better than the three marks.

- Writing experimentally. If your novel sounds like poetry, it's probably not good poetry. Or good prose, either.

- Using cute quote marks. As in "She was a karate expert, a real 'knock-out.'" See what's at work there? The author is winking at you from behind the narrative, telling you he's made a funny, wanting you to notice it. Take off the quotes, and the irony is still there. Let the reader apply his own standards to how funny it is. Stick to using quote marks exclusively to fence in your dialogue.

- Stepping into the story. The reason this device is so funny in the old Woody Allen movies is because it's so outrageous. But don't write expressions in which the author intrudes in the fictional world: "If she only knew what was waiting for her on the other side of that door"; and "he was wrong"; or "little did she know." I groaned to see this goofy tic used in both *The Help* and the latest Jack Reacher novel by Lee Child. Only once, but it was enough to jar the mojo of a reader.

Check out Elmore Leonard's *10 Rules of Writing*. You can Google it. You can find it as a book on Amazon. You'll see some similarities between his list and mine. For that matter, between his list and *The Elements of Style*. And do Google Mark Twain's essay, "Fenimore Cooper's Literary Offenses."

Bottom Line: You're trying to engage readers, not enrage them. I used to advise writers to *Write to suit yourself.* That was exactly wrong. Truly, we people do think about ourselves, but a writer who wants to attract the attention of others—many others—must put his interests aside and consider the answer to the question every reader asks: Why should I care? Or, what's in this for me? It's that business about PARTICIPATIONS?".

Evaluate Your Opener Incident for Reading Ease and Reader Participation

> *Revising your first Incident by modeling the techniques of best-selling authors—using tools that will help you reinvent your writing.*

Here's what you're going to do in chapter 6:

- Edit your Opener Incident using numeric goals as a guide.
- Inject precision into your novel by choosing the right words.
- Take the first steps to reinvent your writing style.
- Scan your Opener for greater reading ease and participation.
- Write more compact Incidents, starting with your very next one.

EDIT LIKE A PRO

You have sketched at least two Incidents and written one in draft, right? Time to edit the first Incident. I'll just assume it's your Opener.

Let's brainstorm with the likes of John Grisham, Stephen King, Terry McMillan, Anna Quindlen, Danielle Steel, and other best-selling authors.

While tossing around some crazy ideas a few years ago, looking for new ways to revise and edit my writing, I studied success. And not just a single case of success or success in only the things I read. But success all across the board. I chose my favorite author and my least favorite. I chose women and men, and their ratings new and old. My sole criterion: Best-selling authors only need apply.

The authors and books I chose: Fannie Flagg (*Fried Green Tomatoes at the Whistle Stop Cafe*), Kaye Gibbons (*Ellen Foster*), John Grisham (*The Street Lawyer*), Jan Karon (*A New Song*), Stephen King (*Misery*), Elmore Leonard ("Hanging Out at the Buena Vista," a short story), Terry McMillan (*How Stella Got Her Groove Back*), Anna Quindlen (*One True Thing*), Danielle Steel (*Star*), and Wallace Stegner (*Angle of Repose*).

Two questions for you: Besides being best-sellers, what traits are common to the works of these authors? Of the traits I've listed here, which do you think are decisive?

- Active voice
- Short words
- Short sentences
- Short paragraphs
- Short tempers
- Short literary agents

You likely want to know: Why would I choose the romance novels of Danielle Steel next to *Angle of Repose* by Wallace Stegner, which won the Pulitzer Prize?

To be honest, I don't know why I put them side by side at first. Except that *Angle of Repose* is my favorite novel, and I wanted to compare it to something less favorite. I am not a fan of Danielle Steel, but I know that at the time of my study, she wrote one or two novels a year, and all of her novels hit the top of the charts. I respect success, and I wanted to learn how and why Ms. Steel earned it each time she put out a new book.

So I took that pair of writers and eight more. I turned three writing samples from each into text files on my computer. The samples ranged from 1,500 to 2,000 words—except for the full Elmore Leonard short story, which ran to fewer than 900 words. As a form of control, I took the first one-third of each sample from the opening paragraphs of each novel. I also took a second sample beginning at the first full paragraph on the center page of the novel. For the third sample, I went to the back of the book in each case and tried to find a piece with high-energy content. If I had a bias, I knew it would show up here.

Before comparing the samples, I also took selections from some not so best-selling authors. I also used a novel that an unpublished author sent me. I sampled a Medal of Honor citation from a government manual, too. It's not fiction, but I used it because it describes combat actions that any credible fiction writer could have turned into high-energy writing. I used a sample of my second *Force Recon* novel, which my editor had not yet marked up.

All told, I used more than 20,000 words, a file about a fourth the size of a novel. If you were to conduct the same study, you might choose best-selling authors or titles on today's lists. But I'll bet you would get the same results.

And those results were?

The pros most often used short words, short sentences, short paragraphs, and active voice. You guessed that already from my list. Now let's look at the style of the pros. Let's see what they have in common. And let's take the first steps to reinvent your writing.

In reverse order, let's look at each element and see how each comes into play.

THE WINNING QUALITIES OF BEST-SELLING NOVELISTS

ACTIVE VOICE. As a rule, the best-selling writers tend to use the active voice.

Remember our lesson on the active voice from the last chapter? One more example, from *Moonlight in Odessa*:

> I bit my lip.

The actor in the sentence, I, is placed before the verb and acts, bit, on a receiver of the action, my lip.

Here's the passive construction:

> My lip was bitten by me.

Now, Janet Skeslien Charles would never write that ridiculous line. And I do so only as a teaching point, to remind you of the word order: The receiver of the action, my lip, stands ahead of the verb, and the actor follows the verb.

Unless you are using the passive with purpose, that is, to mellow out a passage, to avoid giving blame for an action, to make a sentence sing a softer melody, or to slow down the pace of your novel, always use the active voice. Which is to say, use the passive voice only when you have a purpose. Using the active voice most of the time will elevate your writing beyond—far beyond— the run-of-the-mill office writer. But by itself, use of the passive is not an issue that separates the amateurs from the pros.

SHORT PARAGRAPHS AND SHORT SENTENCES. Except for one huge—and artful—sentence by Terry McMillan, which ran to 171 words, in general, the pros average a sentence length of fourteen words. Danielle Steel goes to sixteen, and Terry McMillan to eighteen, same as the government sample. But that one hefty sentence skews McMillan's average. Besides, every good writer varies sentence length.

Let's talk about sentences for a bit. What makes a sentence work? In a word, comprehension. No matter how creative and poetic your writing, if a reader struggles with it, your poetry might as well be a diseased elm falling in an empty forest. We're talking participation. So if that ever goes down, you want to first draw a crowd to watch it fall, and maybe run away in panic. Focus on comprehension as we talk about writing style. Choose precise words. How you put those works together is called effective writing.

One factor affects sentence comprehension more directly than any other. Simplicity. And nothing contributes to simplicity like brevity. The shorter a sentence, the greater the chance a reader will understand it. Period.

When I taught basic reporting to military journalism students for the Department of Defense, I came across a scale that measured how newspaper readers understood sentences of varying length. I don't remember the source of the study and I haven't been able to dig it up in my research. But because it had such an effect on me, I remember it so clearly I can reproduce it here with no trouble.

SENTENCE COMPREHENSION

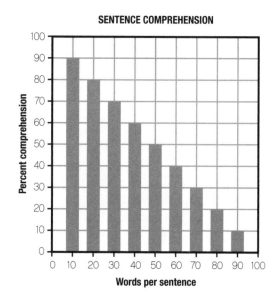

YOU CAN WRITE A NOVEL

At one extreme left, the scale tells you that a reader will understand a one-word sentence 99 to 100 percent of the time. At the other extreme, readers can decipher a one-hundred-word sentence at the 1 percent level or less.

Am I saying you should write fiction full of one-to two-word sentences? Hardly. Close your eyes. Can you still see the scale?

Of course you can. You can thank me later for putting that tattoo on your brain. You now have a tool you will never forget. From now on, every time you write a sentence, you will call up that picture and do the math.

If the sentence you just wrote comes to twenty words, what percent of your readers will get your point? You say 80 percent? Nice work. If you write fifty-word sentences—all other things being equal—how many readers will get your point? About half, right? Are you happy about that? If you dare to write seventy-five-word sentences, you know what you can expect to achieve. Beware.

SHORT WORDS. Here's the key at last. Use short words to keep readers engaged. No other trait ties my author study group together more strongly. And when those writers are put up against not-so-best-selling authors, the result will dazzle you. Best-selling authors in my study average words of 4.21 letters. The amateur, the government writer, and beginning novelists like you average a little more than five letters per word.

Not dazzled? As a naked number you might think one more letter per word is small change. Hardly. Only when you begin editing the words that make up the number in your writing sample do you realize how critical it is to revision and editing. Small words matter.

When you edit, nothing boosts a reader's access to your writing like cutting words down to size.

Don't take my word. Prove it to yourself. Take a sample of your writing, say, five hundred words from your Opener Incident. Run a reading ease test on it using the *Check Spelling and Grammar* tool in Microsoft Word. You may have to set up Word to give your stats.

Here's how to set up your program to give you statistics: You may have to set up your program in the preferences for Word. Type the term, readability statistics, into the search field of your Help feature. You'll get this as one of the top items for all but the newest versions of Word:

> On the Tools menu, click Options and then click the Spelling and Grammar tab.

> Select the Check grammar with spelling check box.

Select the Show readability statistics check box, and then click OK.

On the standard toolbar click Spelling and Grammar.

When Microsoft Word finishes checking spelling and grammar, it displays information about the reading level of the document.

Remember that excerpt on page 24 from *Gone Tomorrow*? It begins: *The list is twelve points long* … Here are its Readability Statistics, with those stats I deem most important in bold.

READABILITY STATISTICS	
Counts	
Words	**79**
Characters	338
Paragraphs	4
Sentences	11
Averages	
Sentences per Paragraph	2.8
Words per Sentence (WPS)	**7.2**
Characters per Word (CPW)	**4.1**
Readability	
Passive Sentences (PV)	**0%**
Flesch Reading Ease (FL)	**84.9**
Fleshc-Kincaid Grade Level (F-K)	**3.1**

Reading level stats you care about include a word count, the number of paragraphs, the number of sentences, the average words per sentence, average number of letters in your words, the percentage of passive voice in the sample, and reading level using two scales, Flesch and Flesch-Kincaid. Flesch measures reading ease on a scale of 0 to 100, the higher the number the easier the sample is to read. Flesch-Kincaid measures on a scale of 1 to 12, like grade levels in school. The lower the number, the easier it is to read.

I shy away from the term "grade levels" because I don't want you to think that writing that scores a three on Flesch-Kincaid sounds as if it came out of a third-grade textbook. That's not the case at all. But if it helps you to fix the concept in your head, by all means, fix it, then forget it. Now let's move onto your own little test of your writing genius.

FIND THE KEY EDITING TRAIT

If you haven't already kept the stats, test the reading level of your five-hundred-word sample again and record them.

Copy the five-hundred-word sample and paste it four times below your master sample.

Label the first copy of the master: *Shorter sentences*. Then edit that file. Add periods and question marks. All you're doing is making more sentences. Make no other changes, even if the edited version doesn't make quite the sense you'd like it to.

When you are done, select the sample and run another reading level test. Record the results. Compare those results to the original. Did the Flesch go up and Flesch-Kincaid go down just by using shorter sentences?

Label the next copy of the master: *Shorter paragraphs*. Add a few random returns here and there. Again, no need to make sense. Just leave the rest of the sample alone. Run the reading level test. Record the results. Again, compare.

Label the next copy of the master: *Passive to active voice*. Change all instances of passive voice to active. Leave the rest of the sample alone. Run. Record. Compare.

Label the next copy: *Shorter words*. Do your best to cut every long word down to size. Make no other changes. This might take a while. But it's a great exercise. Run. Record. Compare.

If you like, edit again to get better reading ease levels. Run. Record. Put all your results side by side. If I'm right, you got the best reading levels after cutting words down to size.

Just for the heck of it, copy and paste your sample once again. Edit again, this time using each of the editing methods, but do have the copy make sense. Record your result. Compare that final result to each of the others. I'll bet this version was best of all.

Congratulations. You now have a sense for how the REI can work for you. Very shortly we'll put some numbers to the index and make it help your writing sing.

I hope you also have a sense of how your brain works during the editing process. I hope you felt engaged in your writing as you tried to meet my demand.

SET SOME CREATIVITY GOALS

I have this theory about the brilliance of poets. The demands of meter and rhyming force the poet to reorder words and invent new ones. It's a case where, ironically, rules nourish and perhaps even *require* invention. If I'm right about that, then Shakespeare, already a genius, had to expand that genius to fit the iambic pentameter, rhyme, and other conventions of the dramas of his age.

Whoa.

Did I just say that rules expand your creativity? Do I mean that rules can make your novel better than just writing by the seat of your pants?

Indeed. Depending on whose stats you believe, Shakespeare, with a vocabulary of twenty-one thousand words, invented up to eight thousand words of his own. Granted, he gets credit for words that somebody else might have invented but whose works didn't stay in print for centuries. But let's not argue about that, shall we? Let's just say that there were times when he was in a hurry, couldn't find the right word in his rhyming dictionary or even inside his head, and just pulled something out of thick air.

Which leads me to say that if you follow no rules but just fly by the seat of your pants, then no rules apply. No matter what the level of your native genius, you never force yourself to press the limits of your creativity.

Think about one of the most common rules in publishing: *Cut it to length.* Editors say that all the time. They say it to me every time I write a book. Yes, this one, too.

Now if an editor told you to cut your 500-word sample by 10 percent to 450 words, that's a rule. You don't obey; you don't get into print. Her rule forces you to flex your brain muscle. Expand your creativity. See how that works?

Cut your 500-word sample by 10 percent. Paste another copy of your revised 500-word sample. Edit using any and all of the methods from before until you improve your work to the 450-word count. Don't stop until the sample is 450 words or fewer. As you do this, step outside your mind and body and take note of how you feel as you work. Watch what's going on inside your head.

Finished?

And how did you feel? Did you feel a focus? Did you realize that the distractions of sight and sound didn't bother you as much as they might? Did you lose yourself in the process of working on your words? In case you don't know it, that's what's called getting into the flow. Athletes call it getting into the zone. It's a great place to be, and this tool puts you right there.

Test The Reading Level

Most likely you boosted the reading levels as you cut words, sentences, and paragraphs.

Now, to the larger teaching point. That feeling you get when you are panning for literary gold in the pools and rivulets of your mind? It's the same feeling that the poets go through to get words to fit a metric pattern or either to rhyme or to write blank verse that sings. It's genius at work inside your own head.

Based on this feeling, I invented an editing tool.

THE FICTION WRITER'S READING EASE IDEAL

The Reading Ease Ideal, REI for short, forces you to push the envelope of your genius. It gives you writing goals in simple numbers. And you can test those numbers as many times as you want with the help of a computer program. It forces you to dig deeply to find the right word that will build precision into your writing. It will simplify sentences as well as words.

It will reinvent the way you write. It will take you to another, higher level, no matter what level you're at right now. *The easier it is to read your writing, the greater the reader participation you will achieve. More readers will play a part in your story because you have lowered the barriers.*

Based on my study of the ten novelists I tested, I set an ideal for myself.

And I don't have to tell you, but I will:

REI by the Numbers

When I edit my fiction I want to arrive at:

- No more than 15 word per sentence in any Incident, fewer in high-energy Incidents.

- No more than 4.5 characters a word in any Incident. And fewer in high-energy Incidents.

- No more than 5 percent use of the passive voice. And zero percent in high-energy Incidents.

- No less than 80 percent readability on the Flesch scale. And no less than 90 percent in high-energy Incidents.

- A max of the sixth-grade reading level on the Flesch-Kincaid scale. And less in high-energy Incidents.

In summary, here's the REI.

THE READING EASE IDEAL (REI) MS WORD

Use these goals as a guide for editing and revision

Words per Sentence (avg.) (WPS): 15 maximum

Characters per Word (avg.) (CPW): 4.5 maximum

Passive Sentences (PV): 5% maximum

Flesch Reading Ease (FL): 80 minimum

Flesch-Kincaid Grade Level (F-K): 6 maximum

What This Method Can Teach You About Editing Your Work

Even if you argue that reading ease and characters-per-word are artificial devices, I can counter that imposing the ideal has raised my ability to edit and revise. This editing tool forces you to:

FOCUS ON A CLEAR STANDARD. You can measure your editing progress with it. When your readability falls to 50 percent in a high-action Incident, you sense that it drags. When you pep it up to 79 percent, you give it legs. When you pump it into the 90s, you know it sings. You don't have to rely on some subjective scale like: *It sounds good to me.* You edit by the numbers, and evaluate your genius with the help of a little math.

CUT OUT YOUR DARLINGS. When you get down to the nitty-gritty as you reach a lower word count, you will be more willing to cut your lovely purple phrases. You will, as Paul Verlaine said, "Take eloquence and wring its neck." Because, by now, if you buy into my system, you realize that in best-selling writing, it's not the poetry that counts, but the participation. The more you use the system, the more you realize: *It ain't art; it's bidness.*

ELEVATE YOUR AWARENESS OF PACING. When two characters sit around with drinks, talking about how to set up the tricks and traps of their plot to ruin somebody's marriage, you know you can ease off on word length and allow some use of the passive voice. When a couple gets into a dogfight, you know you must dial up the action. Short words and short sentences lead to high energy and fast action. The REI acts as a guide as you ramp up the energy in an Incident. Once again, you can measure progress. In fact you can control the energy level. There's no better pacing tool. No more seat-of-the-pants decisions. Now you can adjust pacing by the numbers.

EXPLORE WORD CHOICES. When words like *dependability* and *extrapolations* grind your scores into the dust, you will find precise, short words. *Rock-solid creds* and *hunches.* Or else you will cut the monsters from the page.

IDENTIFY DETOURS AND ASIDES. When either the writer or a character flies off on a tangent, this tool will shine a light on the sin of overwriting. Once you see it, you can fix it.

MANAGE WORD COUNT. I don't know if you have this problem, but when I write, I always blow the word count off the charts. To me, editing means adding. Improving means filling in blanks. But with this tool, I can see where to fix things, not fatten them in the final draft. You'll have to try it. You'll see.

WRITE WITH ECONOMY. This might be the best effect of all. The pain and shame of such fat early drafts made me want to write leaner prose the next time around.

CREATE DISTINCTIVE CHARACTERS. On second thought, maybe *this* is the best effect of all. You can apply the scan to various characters and allow the college profs and lawyers in your stories to speak at a denser level. The kid from an East L.A. gang will talk with short words, slang, short sentences.

If your word program doesn't have a readability test, no problem. Millions of computers do have them, and you can carry your novel around on disk looking for one to rent or borrow. It's worth the effort. You can also find a free analysis tool at www.usingenglish.com. You can become a member for free and that gives you access to the more advanced statistics at the *Text Analysis & Statistics* link up to about twenty thousand words. The site lacks a passive voice tool, but it does have some great tutorials to teach you how to recognize and convert passive voice to the active. If you're on a budget, this site will work for you.

RUN THE REI SCAN ON YOUR OPENER

Now. Let's take the first giant step to reinvent your writing. Run a scan on your Opener.

Then, edit your Incident until it meets every goal of the REI Index.

Your goal is a simple plan: *Make it easy, by the numbers, for your reader to read.*

The easier it is the greater the chances that the reader will feel as if he's playing a part in your story. He's racing through to see what happens next. She's turning pages at an insane pace. When she reviews your book, she will say in the reader review section on Amazon and other sites that you wrote a page turner. Get ready to feel the brain sparks as your genius kicks in. Talk about fun. A few tips:

1. **Do NOT run a reading ease scan on your entire novel** all at once. The software will give you overall reading ease statistics, but you will find them a waste of time for a novel of 100,000 words. Entire sections of your fiction might be boring dreck full of passive musings and a reading ease at the doctorate level. At times you might have crisp Incidents of high-energy dialogue and fast action. The two might average out to meet the ideal standards you set for yourself, but the dreck will earn rejections for you. So …

2. **Work with one Incident at a time.** One Incident or chapter. And don't worry about pacing or blowing away the standard just because this is a high-energy Incident. Pacing comes later. For now, all you're doing is editing.

3. **Optional: Evaluate your favorite writers in the genre in which** you plan to publish. As you saw, my chosen writers and their novels came from different genres and varying literary acclaim. You might select two novels apiece by five romance writers if you plan to write romances. Or you might choose five thrillers by the same author. Just make sure they are best-sellers. Run a scan on their work. Use the results to set a standard you want to meet. Mind you, I'm not saying you should copy another writer. Just that you should adopt the tools and newly revealed secrets of his success to your own fiction.

4. **Caution: Make a backup.** *Before* you work your editing magic on a copy, **create a master file of the original version** of your fiction. That way if you cut too deeply, you can refer to the master and restore selections.

5. **Some reading ease software lets you turn off certain** grammar and punctuation checks like Microsoft Word. Do turn those off, except for the feature that checks passive constructions. That way, the scan will work faster.

6. **Create a log** and enter your results each time you edit and rerun your own scan. It doesn't have to be complex. You could do it in a spreadsheet, but a yellow pad of paper will work just as well with you writing

the numbers in pencil. The main point is you'll be able to chart your progress with each version and adjust to meet the goals.

7. **If you feel like I'm pushing you into a box, relax.** We won't rely on reading ease and math results alone at the expense of your lyrical genius. In this first round of edits use all the usual editing tips you learned in school, on the job, from your own research, and from writing seminars and this book. At this stage, just meet the goals in the REI stats. We'll come back to your work later in the revision process with new tools and new tips for pumping up the tone, voice, music, and poetry in your writing overall.

There you go. Short chapter. Long on work, though, eh? And for your reader participation, I think long on results.

■ Create the Rest of Your Main Story Line
■ as a Series of Headlines

> *Writing your second most important incident into the novel, then your third, and ...*

Here's what you're going to do in chapter 7:

- Create the rest of your central story line—structuring the easy way.
- Write your Point-of-No-Return Incident.
- Develop the Closer Incident further.
- Apply the simplest of structures to Incidents, *Tragedy Versus Triumph.*

YOUR NOVEL'S STORY LINE

We build the structure of your main story line as a series of chapters or Incidents. In the old days, I called this a scene card, which, as you know does not exist anymore. We're dealing with Incidents for the rest of your writing life. In this book, we keep track of our separate Incidents using the Incident checklist. As with each character's dossier, the headline of each Incident will expand into a full-blown list. As before, you can download this structure file from my Website, www.*writefromparadise.com*

✚ Chapter or Incident—Headlines Only

✚ Opener Incident (A)—Headlines Only

✢ Chapter or Incident—Headlines Only

✢ Chapter or Incident—Headlines Only

✢ PoNR Incident (D)—Headlines Only

✢ Chapter or Incident—Headlines Only

✢ Chapter or Incident—Headlines Only

✢ Chapter or Incident—Headlines Only

✢ Chapter or Incident—Headlines Only

✢ Chapter or Incident—Headlines Only

✢ Closer Incident (Z)—Headlines Only

✢ Chapter or Incident—Headlines Only

Don't get upset if this doesn't look the way you think it should. You see an Incident before the Opener and after the Closer (Z), where no letters of the alphabet can be. And you might expect to write more chapters or Incidents. Or fewer. Or a given chapter might have distinct Incidents within. No problem. As before, you can copy and paste as many chapters or Incident titles and put them where you wish. You can also move an Incident, such as the PoNRI up or down in Outline View of Microsoft Word.

Caution 1: As before, perform a Save As with this file and rename it as in, *Slumdog_Central_Story_Line*. Keep the master for copying when you get to your next novel.

Caution 2: Also as before, in Outline View with all levels collapsed as you see them above, copy that string of five headings below the words, "PoNRI (D) ..." Then move your cursor to the bottom of the file and paste from the clipboard. Later, when you want to insert an Incident, you can move down and grab one of those and move it up. Or copy just one, if you please. Your call.

One cool thing: In that group of five or ten you just pasted, select one collapsed line "Chapter or Minor Incident ..." and with it highlighted, select your a font color that is not the default black. Select another heading and give it a second font color.

Do this three or four times, each time using a different color. Later, when you begin to write subplots, we'll organize each color into a string of those

Incidents into a coherent story line of its own, then place each into its proper spot in the story. Then using our writer brilliance, we'll weave them seamlessly into the plot.

For now though, we are only going to work on a central story line, the spine of your novel.

As you know if you've seen any of my earlier books, I don't use the word outline, except to talk about *Outline View* in Word. Telling people to outline their plot scares them off.

One more thing before we begin to place our Incidents in the central story line. Double-click on one of the plus signs for an incident that you might want either to explore or to add data.

I had a motive in turning you loose back in chapter 2 to sketch your Opener and Closer. A writer's native energy can inspire her to start writing a novel. Getting started is never the problem. It's keeping your mojo that can give you a migraine. Sometimes you run out of ideas. Sometimes you flat just don't know where next to go. That's why there are so many first chapters in the lives of would-be authors. But we can fix that. In fact, you may find yourself taking first chapters out of notes all over your house, using this system to reengineer them, firing up the boilers of your genius to finish them.

This is where I step in, to tidy up and put your mind to rest. I'm here to ignite that little blue flame of your genius, the pilot light. You'll turn up the gas when you're ready. My logic is easy to master if you do it one step at a time. So try this for starters.

If it's not already done, in Outline View, collapse all the levels to Level 1. You do this either by clicking the plus sign next to each main heading that is expanded or you click on the little black upside down triangle at the center of the Outline View task bar and choose "Show Level 1."

We are just going to write a few headlines for starters.

TIPS FOR WRITING INCIDENT HEADLINES

Stick to the main story line. Just write the headlines for what happens between your main characters as they go about facing off the central conflict in your novel. If an unrelated Incident or subplot or plot twist asserts itself out of nowhere, mark it as a note on the page with a symbol like +++, @@@, or ###, so you can find it later. Put it aside and get back to the main story line. At all costs, stay focused.

By the way, running down those symbols is a good activity when you think you've run up against writer's block. Just start making fixes and you'll soon find yourself back in the flow of writing.

- **Be brief about it.** Get as much of the story down as quickly as possible in a rough story sequence. Work fast. Write headlines only. Work as if you are writing notes on your hand just before stepping up to the lectern to give a speech. You can come back later to expand upon your headlines, literally as we expand the Incident headline.

- **Keep moving.** From Incident to Incident. If you find yourself stymied, skip over any difficulties and get to the next place you can pick up the story. Fill in the gaps later.

- **But don't sacrifice any gems of genius.** A great idea might whack you upside the head as you're scribbling headlines for Incidents. Capture as much as you need to, of course. Expand that incident heading and plug in details, if you must. Or, if you write a five-hundred-word headline, simply expand the heading by using a couple of returns to create one or more paragraphs in your five hundred words of text. Then use the green arrows in the outlining task bar to select "Body Text" or some other level. Doing so will push the text, or *demote* it, to use the proper term, that is, hide it from sight when "Level 1" is selected.

- **Keep it informal.** For now, forget about grammar and choosing the perfect word from a thesaurus. Remember to spill your tale as if you were telling a friend about a movie you've just seen: "The T rex breaks through the fence, and the goofy lawyer tries to hide in the restroom. The T rex makes a meal of him right off the toilet." I'd use those very words.

I'm guessing that sketching your story like this will give you anywhere from ten to fifty headlines. Depends on how well you can stick to a task. Or how many times a crackling line of dialogue strikes you in the ear, telling you to capture it. In which case, you'll expand the Incident and jot down your thoughts inside the checklist. Nothing wrong with that. Even if this happens, continue going back to the writing of Incident headlines until the story begins to take shape, no matter how rough.

Don't worry about whether a Incident is major or minor, whether you will turn it into a chapter, or whether you expect to write only a few hundred words. Just keep going. And don't even think about cementing the sequence of your Incidents with superglue. You're working in clay, not granite. The great thing about the digital file in Outline View is that you can move the events, dragging them higher or lower in the sequence of the story with a few clicks of the mouse. And as ideas occur to you, you will come back to the story line and add Incidents as you need them.

Above all, feel the sense of freedom this system gives you. As long as you save your files often, you have nothing to fear.

YOUR PIVOTAL COMPLICATIONS—TRIUMPH VERSUS TRAGEDY

Anytime in the course of a novel that the story changes direction because of problems introduced or complications resolved between master characters, write it as an Incident. Your novel should never stand still. A static story is a dead story. Your Incidents should move either toward triumph or tragedy at all times. A sudden reversal on that path, a pivot, sets the story flying in the opposite direction. Jamal the *Slumdog Millionaire* wins all that money, which is a triumph. But he goes straight to jail and torture, clearly a tragedy. In the film, Jamal sees Latika, the woman he loves on the train platform. It appears that they will get together, but as he watches, the moment of triumph is stolen from him. Triumph pivots to tragedy. Tragedy pivots to triumph.

On the other hand, the moment you find yourself squirming in your seat at a movie, you know the story is stagnant. The instant you catch yourself bored in writing your own story, your genius is whispering in your mind's ear that your writing is static.

That's the point at which any writer should worry. If you are bored with your own story, imagine a reader sitting in an easy chair. Imagine that your novel has just inspired her to put down your book and step away from it. She has just remembered that she has to go outside and watch the grass grow. All together now, *shudder*.

The Structure of Slumdog Millionaire

I'll give you a quick review of the structure of *Slumdog Millionaire*, the novel originally titled *Q&A*. It's a simple plan. Remember, we already wrote the first headline in the last chapter. The others are the chapter headings right out of the book.

- ✛ Opener (A) (PoNRI)—Jamal jailed for winning millions on a quiz show
- ✛ Chapter 1 Incidents—1,000 Rupees—Salim's hero revealed as a pervert
- ✛ Chapter 2 Incidents—2,000 Rupees—The Burden of a Priest
- ✛ Chapter 3 Incidents – 5,000 Rupees—The Brothers Promise
- ✛ Chapter 4 Incidents—10,000 Rupees—A Thought for the Crippled
- ✛ Chapter 5 Incidents—50,000 Rupees—How to Speak Australian
- ✛ Chapter 6 Incidents—100,000 Rupees—Hold on to Your Buttons
- ✛ Chapter 7 Incidents—200,000 Rupees—Murder on the Western Express
- ✛ Chapter 8 Incidents—500,000 Rupees—A Soldier's Tale
- ✛ Chapter 9 Incidents—1,000,000 Rupees—License to Kill
- ✛ Chapter 10 Incidents—10,000,000 Rupees—Tragedy Queen
- ✛ Chapter 11 Incidents—100,000,000 Rupees—X Gkrz Opknu (Or a Love Story)
- ✛ Chapter 12 Closer Incidents (Z)—1,000,000,000 Rupees—The Thirteenth Question
- ✛ Epilogue Incidents

Granted, the author's chapter titles after chapter 1 don't help you very much as headlines, but I can't spoil the plot for you. Even if you saw the film, the novel, as I've said, is a story of its own. The structure within each chapter is simply a review of an Incident in Jamal's life. Then the author details a second Incident in the chapter, telling what happens on the set of the game show, Jamal's responses, and his conflict with the show host, Prem. Between those two Incidents is usually a brief segue, a few words passed between Jamal and his lawyer.

Which makes this as good a point as any to tell you the obvious: Within any chapter or many major Incident, you should feel free to write any number of other Incidents, major or minor. In the early stages of my story lines,

I tend to keep to major Incidents. After I have set the entire story down, I find it easier to see gaps that I have to fill with Incidents of lesser importance. I also find that many times I can write from one major Incident to another with only a few words of narration.

Best of all, I'm happy when I can get from one Incident to another with no words at all between. One Incident ends. The other Incident begins. Readers are smart. Thanks to movies, they see passenger jets taking off, they blink, and those jets land. But they don't even need that much. An Incident ends with your hero in New York. The next Incident opens with him standing ankle-deep in the Pacific as the sunset winks out. No need to take him—or your reader—through passenger screening.

Another thing you may notice is that in the list on the previous page, you find the PoNRI inside the Opener. Seem odd? Not really. The PoNRI is really what happened in the first nine words of the novel, remember? *I have been arrested. For winning a quiz show.*

The Point of No Return took place in the backstory. Jamal's life is never going to be the same. If you or I had been writing this, we might have handled it differently. We might have set up his answering one of the questions on the game show, then cut to instant tragedy in the torture room. In fact, that's how Simon Beaufoy portrays it in his screenplay.

Novelist Vikas Swarup chose to open his story at the police station. I think he did just fine. He lost nothing.

But let's leave *Slumdog Millionaire* behind us for now. Let's put you to work scratching out a few headlines for your own novel.

I think we're already clear that your Opener should be a Chapter Incident. And you have a rough idea of where to put two other Chapter Incidents, your PoNRI, Your Closer, and the Climax of Your Novel. It's as simple as ADZ, right?

I have a few words for the D and the Z of this process. Let's talk about the PoNRI and the Closer.

FIND AND CRAFT YOUR POINT-OF-NO-RETURN INCIDENT

In most novels, this is the complication that bridges the setup and middle of your novel. Let me give you one line from a terrific film to illustrate a PoNRI, a line that almost everybody in America knows and uses about three times a day: **"Houston, we've had a problem."**

Really now, do you need any more than that? From the moment astronaut James Lovell uttered those words after launch (or was it when Tom Hanks said them in the movie, *Apollo 13*?), you knew nothing in that mission, or the film, was going to be the same. It was a point of no return for all time. If these guys can't find a way to guide their spacecraft around the moon and back to earth, they're going to fly straight out of the solar system.

Those words, usually spoken as, "Houston, we have a problem," entered the lexicon forever as well. In fact, if you'll forgive the aside, Prem, the game show host in *Slumdog Millionaire*, the novel, uses the expression in the studio after a glitch with some spotlights. And our hero in a moment of supreme irony and surprise, the kid, who has been winning money by the fistful because he is a font of facts, doesn't realize what Prem means.

Since this example illustrates so well, let's draw some lessons for writing your own PoNRI.

Essentials of a PoNRI Complication

Usually once your novel's Opener sets the direction for your story, things begin falling into place—or falling apart, creating a sense of the inevitable. Suppose your heroine is a reluctant bank robber. Once she's inside the bank, in front of the security cameras with bullets flying, nothing in that story can ever be the same.

STRONG, BELIEVABLE MOTIVATIONS AND ACTIONS. Coincidence alone won't bring about an Incident this critical. You must create a sense of the inevitable.

A STRONG SENSE OF SUSPENSE. Even if they're playing in a romantic comedy, your characters must feel trapped in the morass of the PoNRC. In *The Help*, the PoNRI is simply installing a toilet for the maid. The decision. The process. The construction. The use. You feel a quickening of pulse and shortness of breath at the outrage some characters feel.

A CRUCIAL DECISION POINT. Because of the situation that unfolds in your PoNRC Incident, the heroic characters must make choices that affect the novel all the way through to the climactic Incident and its logical ending. Often a heroic character will make a wrong choice because he thinks it will solve all the problems he's created so far; instead he's created a new set of quandaries.

Final words on your point-of-no-return complication: Don't worry about it. You may even disguise a heroic character's fateful decision by downplaying it. Later, the reader will enjoy a wondrous moment of discovery when the importance of that decision dawns. So, if your PoNRC doesn't hit you between the eyes right now, just move on to the next step. Sooner or later, it will make its appearance. You will know it when you see it.

Write Your PoNRI.

Double-click on the plus sign to expand the PoNRI headline. Then, in the center of the task bar, select "Show Level 2". That helps us focus on only one part of the checklist. Build this Incident in three parts, beginning, middle, end, just as you did your Opener.

Once you've finished, run this PoNRI through the REI scan and edit a copy of it until you meet all the goals (to refresh your memory, see chapter 6). Then …

WRITE YOUR NEXT INCIDENT

You already have the structure in place, that is, the chapter heads or major Incidents mapped out in something of a triumph versus tragedy scheme. So start on another Incident. And don't worry about writing your novel in sequence.

It's simply a drag to write Incidents to tie your fun Incidents together. Instead, write your most favorite, most fun Incidents first. Doing so will keep up your enthusiasm. Secondly, you may later decide that one or two lines of narration is all you need to take you from one Incident to the next.

In the end (no pun intended), your best Incident, and probably your favorite, will be your Closer. You already have it in sketch form. As you go along writing favorite Incidents, you will now and then expand the Incident checklist for your Closer, detailing new twists, tie backs to earlier event in the story, and ideas for tying up loose ends.

Finally, there will come a moment when you can't put it off any longer, you just have to write it, and more than that, you have to make it the most powerful slam-dunk Incident in the entire novel. And when you do, I have a little checklist for your Closer. Might as well give it to you now.

Incident Z–The All-American Kick-Butt Closer

To quote Stephen R. Covey, author of *The Seven Habits of Highly Effective People*: "Begin with the end in mind."

You wouldn't dream of striking out on a journey to Saco, Montana, the "mosquito capital" of North America without pulling out a map and finding

Saco. Why on earth would you begin a novel without knowing where you'll arrive in the end?

I've suggested writing the Closer first. If you've already written your Opener, sketch this Incident next. Once you know the beginning and ending, it's so much easier to fill in the in-between. Remember the Twain quote about *Deerslayer* arriving in the air, which we discussed back on page 17.

Now, you can argue that true art requires the author to develop strong characters with minds of their own who take the story wherever they want to, all the way to *The End*. In fact in part of her review, one of the Amazon reviewers who didn't like the first edition of YCWAN reports: "If you're a fly-by-the-seat-of-your-pants writer, then this book won't be helpful for you."

I agree, especially if you are selling books already. If you have a system that sells, stick with that—just put down this book and walk away from my system.

The rest of you, ask yourself this: Are you a fly-by-the-seat-of-your-pants reader? I would argue that most readers are not. They don't like formless books or aimless characters. When they start on a journey, they want the bus driver to know where she is going.

If you are the driver of a novel, you want to fill your bus with readers. If you think you can do it by driving by the seat of your pants, go ahead. But do be wary of driving in circles.

Let me put it another way. Readers don't care about your needs or systems. They expect you to deliver an experience. They care about themselves, and this book will help you write to satisfy their first need—themselves—the *me* in each of us.

Remember my question from an earlier chapter? Did *you* buy this book to help *me* make my house payment?

Stick with my system. Sell a few titles. Build your confidence. Hit the big time. Then, by all means, fly away. Seat of your pants and all.

Meanwhile, having the Closer in mind at the outset is crucial to writing your novel. Visualizing the climax gives you a target and keeps your novel on track. It becomes the measure by which you decide to keep an Incident, a paragraph, a sentence, or a word elsewhere in the story. When you're finished writing, the climactic Incident should prove to be the point of the most intense conflict and action, the moment at which all that has come before is aimed, and the point from which the ending is the natural result.

So your All-American Kick-Butt Closer must be even more powerful than your big, fat Greek Opener.

Here's another little checklist whose emphasis once again is on participation:

A Checklist for the Climactic Closer Incident

Your **Closer** is the most important Incident in the novel, bar none. Yes, the **Opener** is critical but only second in importance to the climax. Which is why I made it the largest letter in my ADZ alphabet timeline.

The Opener must impress an agent enough to ask for more pages to help her decide whether to represent your book. The Opener must impress an editor enough to force him to ask for more pages to help him decide whether to buy your book. The Opener must impress the reader to take your book home from the bookstore.

But it's the climax that closes the deal for all three parties—that's one reason I call it the Closer.

Defining the Closer a Bit More Precisely

The question is, when I say Closer do I mean the climax, the resolution, or both? You could make yourself crazy overthinking this point. So let me talk about it by using an example we've already discussed. In the novel, *Gone Tomorrow* by Lee Child, the Opener is six chapters long. And I suppose you could include chapter 7, if you want to, because the seamless structure is like a string of linked subway cars, to coin a phrase. The Opener is the entire content of all those chapters. It's the high action set up to the novel, and it meets all those criteria I talked about. Think of it as a mini novel, if you like. Or one large Incident broken into six or seven smaller Incidents. And within each chapter, you can argue that includes other Incidents. Or tales. Or even tiny tales that you might consider Incidents in their own right. But as I say, don't make yourself crazy. Just keep on telling tales, no matter what you call them.

In the Closer, I include the climactic confrontation, which leads to an inevitable, if not, reasonable resolution. Don't try to get too academic about how many Incidents you should include in your Closer. Very likely, you will take the climax as several Incidents, and the resolution, which follows a shorter one.

Can we leave it at that? At times I feel as if I've already been too prescriptive. I don't want to tell you that your Opener requires a minimum of seven Incidents. Or that a Closer should contain anywhere from two to thirteen.

I can tell you this: The editor who bought my first novel said that after he decided he liked the opening fifty pages, he skipped right to the ending to see if I could deliver in the climax. Only then did he make an offer on the book. He didn't worry too much about the resolution. I doubt many editors do. If you've written a good story, your resolution will write itself.

In any case, I've never forgotten what that first editor told me. It's one reason I tell you to aim your story on a straight line from A to Z.

What readers say after they put your book down matters more for your sales than what they say when they pick it up.

So, ask yourself these questions about your **Closer**:

IS THIS INCIDENT A TITANIC FINAL STRUGGLE? Blow away your readers. Simple as that. No Incident that precedes the Closer should be more exciting. This is the payoff for your fiction.

DOES THE HEROIC CHARACTER CONFRONT THE WORTHY ADVERSARY? Absolutely mandatory. No exceptions.

IS THE CONFLICT RESOLVED IN THE HEROIC CHARACTER'S FAVOR? Not mandatory. But it's usually the most popular choice, meaning most readers like it that way, meaning it's a more commercial choice.

DOES THE HEROIC CHARACTER LEARN AN IMPORTANT LESSON? The most dramatic events of our lives teach our characters (and us) something of lasting value. Our scars cost us something, perhaps innocence or purity, but we also wear them like badges of learning. A reader who walks away from the novel with a *so-what* attitude will kill you in the word-of-mouth department.

DOES THE INCIDENT AVOID COINCIDENCE OR DIVINE INTERVENTION? Your heroic character's decisions and actions must decide the story's most crucial battle. Readers want heroes to act heroically.

DOES THE INCIDENT INTRODUCE NEW MATERIAL? It shouldn't. Everything that appears in the Closer should have been set up earlier in the story. Worse yet, new material introduced by the writer rather than the hero is flat-out cheating. Readers hate that.

DOES THE INCIDENT RELY ON FLASHBACKS? Avoid them at all cost in the Closer. Keep the story moving with action and dialogue.

DOES THE CLOSER USE EXPOSITION? Explanation causes this vital Incident to drag. It's the one thing I hate about parlor mysteries. If the heroine has to give a ten-minute lecture to show how brilliant she is, the story has failed in some way. The genius should be self-evident, both in the heroine and the author's work.

IS THE CONCLUSION LOGICAL? Just as all that goes before should point to the Closer, even if many signposts have been artfully concealed, all that flows from the decisive moment of climax should be reasonable. An ending with a twist is fine, but no tricks.

DOES THE CLOSER LEAVE US FEELING A SENSE OF WONDER? Contrary to the conventional wisdom about impressions, your novel will be judged by its final impression, not its first. What will readers tell their friends after they put down your story?

Bottom line?

You must create a climactic Incident that surpasses any other Incident in the novel in terms of action, conflict, imagery, and dialogue. Blow your readers away with the height and depths of emotions you achieve. Tattoo the outcome of your story on their brains and hearts forever. Leave them feeling disadvantaged that they might never meet your heroic character again (unless, of course, you write another novel featuring her).

It's so important, I've a second checklist for you

Dos and Don'ts for the Last Ten Thousand Words of Your Story

- **Don't introduce any new characters or subplots**. Don't introduce *anything* new. Any appearances within the last fifty pages should have been foreshadowed earlier, even if mysteriously.

- **Don't describe, muse, explain, or philosophize.** In other words, keep the author out of the story, and don't let it drag. By this point in the story, setup is done, complication is wrapping up, and resolution should be entirely uncluttered so you and the reader can make a dash to the finish line. Keep description to a minimum, action and conflict to the max. You have placed all your charges. Now, light the fuse and run.

- **Do create that sense of *Oh wow!*** Once or twice on every page, if possible more frequently. We discussed the notions of novelty and surprise early on. Your best novelties and biggest surprises go here. Readers and film viewers love it when some early, trivial detail plays a part in the finale. One or more of those things will show up here as decisive elements. *Oh wow!*

- **Do enmesh your reader so deeply in the outcome** of your story that she cannot put down your novel to go to bed, to work, or even to the bathroom until she sees how it turns out.

- **Resolve the central conflict.** In favor of your heroic character, if you please. You don't have to provide a happily-ever-after ending, but do try to uplift. Readers want to be uplifted, and editors try to give readers what they want.

- **Don't resort to gimmicks.** No quirky *Twilight Zone* twists or trick endings. No "And then my alarm went off, waking me up to discover the entire story was a dream" or "Why are you asking me? I'm just a dog" jerk-the-reader-around finishes. Nothing cute or stupid. This is no time to be precious. You're at the end of your story, and if people have stuck with you the whole time, it's because you've engaged them, because they have participated. If you insult them in the last pages, that's what they will remember about your novel.

- **Afford redemption to your heroic characters.** No matter how many mistakes she has made along the way, allow the reader—and the character—to realize that, in the end, she has done the right thing.

- **Tie up loose ends of significance.** You don't have to establish a Kodak moment, that rare snapshot in time where every minor issue is neatly solved, but every question you earlier planted in a reader's mind should be addressed, even if the answer is to say that a character will address that issue later, after the book ends.

- **Inject a note of irony, however mild.** Give your audience something to smile about, if only wryly. Is this mandatory? Of course not. But this is a note that covers a lot of territory, in my opinion. Remember the after-movie dancing-in-the-streets moment of *Slumdog Millionaire*? Some would say that that was over the top. I loved it. It was how I felt before I saw them dancing. Even the characters who had died in the film were dancing. Which is to say, ironically, a feeling of happiness, expressed in dancing, transcends squalor, poverty, crime, whatever. I wouldn't recommend an Incident as drastic as that to you as a first-time novelist. I wouldn't recommend against it, either. In any case, I'm probably not the best judge on what is over the top.

- **Tie your final words to events in your Opener.** When you begin a journey of writing a novel, already having established a destination, it's much easier to make calculated detours, twists, and turns in your storytelling tactics. When you reach the ending, go back to insure some element in each of your complications will point to it. It's the tie-back tactic. You don't have to telegraph the finish. Merely create a feeling that the final words hearken to an earlier moment in the story. One of the coolest films of the decade was *The Sixth Sense*, starring Bruce Willis. I suspect that nobody in America saw this film just once. You just had to go back and watch it a second time to enjoy finding all the clues that led to the amazing twist at the end. Or was I the only one?

- **Don't change voice, tone, or attitude.** An ending will feel tacked on if the voice of the narrator suddenly sounds alien to the voice that's been consistent for the previous eighty thousand words.

- **Above all, it's important enough to repeat, do *NOT* introduce cute endings,** visual or language clichés, laborious descriptions, or mysterious, unresolved outcomes. The final impression you want to create is a positive one. Don't leave an audience feeling tricked or cheated.

Well, somebody here has some work to do. If I were you, I'd get busy writing those Incidents. One after another, then the next, then the other. As I've said, write these out of order, if you please, from one favorite to the next. When I work this way, I seldom run out of favorites.

Watch your novel take shape now.

Using subplots and layers, pace, tone, music, and rhythm.

Here's what you're going to do in chapter 8:

- Clean up the mechanics of your novel.
- Apply some advanced revision techniques.
- Create tie backs and transitions.
- Add texture to your story.
- Set your words to music.

REVISE AND PROSPER

Done writing your first draft of the main story line? Excellent.

By now, if you've followed my plan, you have written all your chapter Incidents and other major Incidents, plus any number of smaller Incidents you needed to tie larger Incidents to each other. You have scanned each of them using the Reading Ease Ideal tool in one of the word programs (or a utility online). And you have edited to meet each of the goals in our Reading Ease Index. You have come a long way toward selling a novel. In many ways, especially if you worked in earnest at editing to the REI standards, you will have a novel as good as many in print.

Now let's lift that story to the next level.

Writing is way overrated. Revision counts for far more of the art in any novel. Revision is the money game, the finishing touch. What's the point of dressing your novel and sending it off to New York in a tuxedo if you've left its trouser fly unzipped?

First we'll deal with some mechanics, then some of the tone, voice, music, and poetry in your novel.

MECHANICAL PRELIMINARIES

SPELL-CHECK YOUR INCIDENT. Don't rely on the word processor's spell-checker. Read through your own work to check your spelling as well.

If your software contains a grammar check, remember to turn off all of the punctuation and grammar checks except for passive voice. Then go back and turn on the checks for the categories in which you are the weakest. Is it capitalization? Punctuation? The fewer boxes you check, the faster the program will run. And it will ask you to make fewer changes during the spell-check.

ELIMINATE DOUBLE SPACES BETWEEN WORDS AND SENTENCES. Published novels will not contain two consecutive spaces after sentence punctuation. So eliminate those now and stop typing them into your manuscript if you've been doing so. Another common typo is the use of two spaces between words. Most word processing programs contain a *Find and Change* feature that will correct this error. Allow the program to run until all occurrences of the incorrect spacing have been located and corrected.

UPDATE YOUR CHARACTER PORTFOLIO. A housekeeping detail, but an essential one. Immediately after finishing your first master Incident, update character sheets for anyone who appeared in the Incident. Enter physical and attitudinal details. Modify motivations. Identify distinctive speech patterns, which must remain consistent throughout the novel.

ADD NEW INCIDENTS AS YOU NEED TO. You might find gaps in your story. Only one thing to do. Write new Incidents to fill those gaps. Don't trust your memory to keep track of a new plot idea. Create a new Incident checklist, give it a headline, add enough detail to guarantee you won't forget its essence, and insert it in the proper place in your structure.

TRACK YOUR REVISIONS. Remember way back when I told you to mark revisions or ideas writing your manuscript, using: + + + or @@@ or ###. Use the Find feature now. Check out all the notes you made yourself. Once you make a fix, you want to delete the symbols, so an editor or agent won't read them.

CONDUCT YOUR FINAL RESEARCH. Research a novel after you've begun writing it? Absolutely.

Conduct only enough research to refine your story and remain true to as many facts as you intend to. Some writers—Michael Crichton and Tom Clancy, for instance—relied on research to set the central stage upon which all action plays out. But every writer will bend an inconvenient fact to suit the dramatic purpose of his story. Without getting into wrongs and rights of that, all I'm saying is, research deeply enough to use what you find to the best story-telling advantage. The alternative is to spend (or waste) time collecting details that will never get into a novel. Chances are, if you pack a novel with factual detail, you'll have to explain so much that it will get in the way.

Research only as much as necessary to enrich your novel with reality or, even better, a sense of wonder or discovery. Never include data for its own sake or, worse, to show how brilliant you are.

REVIEW YOUR NUGGET STATEMENT. Take out that summary of your story in thirty-five to forty words, the one you should have kept handy. Does each Incident you've written remain true to the statement? If not, did you lose your focus? Revise the Incident to fit your original purpose—unless that purpose has changed. In which case, revise both your nugget and Incident checklists.

RUN A BUG SWEEP. In the next steps, sweep your Incident, looking for the glitches that are the enemies of selling a manuscript.

HUNT DOWN -LY WORDS AND KILL THEM. Use the "Find" function in your word processor, and look at every single instance of -*ly* in your Incident. Evaluate adverbs one by one:

- Can it be eliminated without changing meaning? If so, do so.
- Is the -*ly* word trying to prop up a weak verb? If so, find a specific power verb to carry the freight.

KILL EXCLAMATION POINTS! Find them. Rid your novel of them. Especially in sentences where you've tried too hard to create a sense of urgency: "The house was afire!" The mark doesn't add a thing to the meaning, except to point out an author's breathless, witless attempt to dramatize. Dramatize with action, not punctuation. Eliminate exclamation points, except in genuine exclamations: "Aha!"

ELIMINATE BODY LANGUAGE. Run the "Find" function again, looking for these types of words one by one:

chuckle	giggle	grin	laugh	smirk
snap	sneer	snort	spat	titter

When you find one used in the form of a quote attribution ("No way," he laughed.), fix it. Okay, if you want to keep *titter*, grant yourself a single use in your novel, but no more.

EDIT SYNONYMS FOR SAID. Sweep your manuscript for the following:

added	admitted	*advised	* affirmed
** agreed	answered	argued	* avowed
claimed	commented	confessed	continued
* declared	emphasized	explained	** joked
maintained	** queried	** quipped	** related
remarked	* replied	reported	revealed

When you find one of these words used to attribute dialogue, replace it with *said*. If *said* seems a poor substitute for a word like *joked*, it's because your line of dialogue isn't carrying the irony you intended to inject. Revise the sentence. By the way, * indicates a particularly objectionable word and ** indicates an utter abomination.

ELIMINATE CLICHÉS. Run a check for *like* and *as*. See if you used them to construct a cliche, as in "quiet as a mouse" or "work like a dog." These are the obvious bugs you can fix at a stroke. Sweep for these cliches as well:

acid test	bad blood	bated breath
beat a hasty retreat	boggles the mind	bound and determined
by the same token	can of worms	dull thud
end of her rope	end result	fell swoop
green with envy	half the battle	hit the sack
lead balloon	lion's share	lock, stock, and barrel
name of the game	nick of time	over a barrel
sick and tired	sickening thud	tail between his legs
ton of bricks	toss and turn	ulterior motive

Entire books have been written to list clichés, but this brief inventory covers some of the most objectionable. Consider which clichés you are most likely to use and search for them.

INVENTORY YOUR ANDS AND BUTS. *And* or *but* sometimes do appear at the beginning of sentences. Few editors will object if you use the device occasionally, but overusing it becomes an affectation and bothersome besides.

SWAT THE "ATOMIC FLYSWATTERS." "Atomic flyswatter" is Theodore M. Bernstein's term for words a writer uses hopefully to inject dull writing with dramatic effect (see his book, *The Careful Writer*). Except in the case where a character uses them in quotes to serve a specific dramatic intent, these words should not appear in your novel:

amazing	divine	awful	dreadful
earthshaking	petrified	mad	sensational
fabulous	stupendous	fantastic	super
frightful	terrible	gorgeous	tremendous
horrible	unbelievable	enormous	wonderful

TERMINATE "..." The dot-dot-dot things (called ellipses) can become bothersome, particularly when used as a device to indicate a pause in dialogue. Never use this technique in your novel. This is not to say it isn't done. ... Professionals do it ... Best-selling writers do ... it. But you can ... turn it into ... a tic ... on the page ... and bug the heck out of an editor in about... three lines.

Why would you want to turn a beautiful story into the typed equivalent of a scratched movie DVD? Answer: You don't.

Question: *Why does the author of YCWAN do it so much?*

Answer: *I can't help it ... I'm weak.*

ELIMINATE PET WORDS. Be honest. Do you find yourself using favorite phrases repeatedly? Find the first use and search for repetitions. Modify such pets so they don't crop up more than once in a manuscript. Create new expressions.

CUT BIG WORDS DOWN TO SIZE. Beyond using the REI, don't be pompous. Mistrust any word five syllables or longer. I'm hoping the REI scan already helped you unearth these things. If not, get to it. Why? Because the reader will think you are arrogant. *Attitudinal? Institutionalize? Recapitulate?* Unless a word like that serves a dramatic purpose (a pompous character says it), don't allow the narrator to use it. As for shorter words, they can be obnoxious, too. Don't use *initiate* when *start* will do. Same with *optimum* versus *best* and *utilize* versus *use*. Be suspicious of all words that end in *-ize* or *-ization.*

ELIMINATE THERE IS AND IT IS. *There's* a bloodsucker. *It's* just as bad. Few words do more damage to a sentence, no matter how innocent they look. Find all instances where you've begun a sentence with *It is* or *It's* or *There is* or *There's*. Recast the sentence, giving it a lifesaving transfusion of action. Instead of "There is a lion ahead. It is running at us," try "A tawny blur streaked toward us, a lion in the attack."

SHUN -ION CONSTRUCTIONS. Another global search. Find words ending in *ion* and see if they're part of mushy sentences: "She asked for the cooperation of the entire department but nobody accepted her recommendation for the adoption of the plan of attack." As opposed to "She asked the entire department to cooperate, but nobody accepted her plan."

KILL WORDS AND PHRASES THAT DESERVE TO DIE. Another list. Run your Incident against words in the first column below. When you hit a match, pick an alternative from the second column.

Four Felonies

in order to	to
for the purpose of	to
in the near future	soon
in the event that	if

And Some Misdemeanors

additional	added, more, other
afford an opportunity	allow, let
approximately	about
at the present time	now
disseminate	issue, send out
due to the fact that	due to, since
endeavor	try
expeditious	fast, quick
facilitate	ease, help
finalize	complete, finish
hopefully	she hoped
impact	effect, change, hit

in conjunction with	with
in regard to	about, on
pertaining to	about, of, on
provide	give, say, supply
retain	keep
therefore, thus	so
and/or	(choose one)
him/her	(choose one)
on or about	(choose one)
etc., et cetera	(don't use)

EDIT DOUBLETS. Edit and revise your manuscript using a little creativity and imagination to cut and eliminate words connected by *and* or *or* when such words and phrases repeat the same idea and concept without enlarging or building upon the meaning and message because they are redundant and repetitive. Get it? Separating such Siamese twins adds punch and vigor to your writing and prose. See what happens when you take a pen or pencil to this very paragraph to cut the *and*s and *or*s and half of each doublet.

Check for these abominations, too: by and by, so-and-so, such and such, this and that, thus and so, yet and still.

DEAL HARSHLY WITH GNATS. Is it *its* or *it's*? Little words that slip through your screens like gnats. Even professional writers sometimes mistype them. Here's a list of bugaboos that can make you look stupid. Run a global search on each one in your completed master Incident. When you find one used incorrectly, stamp it out.

- *Affect* as a verb means "to influence." As a noun it refers to outward appearance. *Effect*, the verb, means "to produce"; the noun is the result produced. "Liquor affects her affect instantly, creating a bizarre effect on her face as it effects change in her behavior." Whew.

- *Alot.* Wrong. Make it two words: *a lot.*

- *Alright.* No, all wrong, *all right*?

- *Like.* As my journalism school professor and mentor, John Bremner, often ranted, *like* is not a conjunction. It's "He worked like a veteran, as a good boy should." Test *like* by mentally replacing it with *similar to* or *similarly to.* If it sounds right, leave *like.* If it doesn't sound sensible, the correct word is *as.* Try it in the example above.

- *Blond* is applied to men, both as an adjective and a noun. "His hair is blond, so he is a blond." Women have more latitude with the adjective. "She has blonde hair" or "she has blond hair." But when used as a noun, "She's always a blonde." Some authorities do not distinguish between the sexes in this manner, but I rather like it.

- *Entitled* refers to a rightful claim. When you put a title on your novel, you *title* it. You never *entitle* a book, a song, or a poem, no matter how often you hear the term misused on radio and television.

- *Farther* refers to literal distances: "He ran a mile farther." Need I say anything *further?*

- *Fewer* is used with countables, my mentor preached, and *less than* with collective quantities. "She has fewer than ten fingers and less than enough sense."

- *Imply* means "to suggest." *Infer* means "to deduce." "From what you imply in your accusation, I infer you'll be pressing charges against me." You'd think that, just by guessing, television writers would get this distinction half the time. But no, they put the wrong word into the actors' mouths every time.

- *Its* is possessive; *it's* is a contraction of *it is.*

- *Loan* is always a noun. To *lend* money is to make a loan. Never let your characters loan money, unless you give them permission to display their ignorance by using the expression in dialogue.

- *Their* is possessive; *they're* is a contraction; *there* is a pronoun.

- *Unique* doesn't allow for degrees of comparison. *More unique, most unique,* and *so unique* are all incorrect.

- *Your* is possessive; *you're* is a contraction of *you are.*

So much for revision by using the global search function on your computer. If you follow these steps, mechanical as they are, you will have eliminated the little bugs that cry out "amateur!" From here on, you're going to have to work at revising some style into your novel.

RUN A STYLE SWEEP

In contrast to the bug sweep, in which you identify mechanical glitches, this sweep guides you in developing a distinctive writing style that will catch an editor's eye.

Take a Stand

Write decisively. You might populate your novel with the occasional wishy-washy character, and even the most heroic character suffers periods of indecision, but you, as an author, cannot indulge in uncertainty.

A novelist who won't take a stand either does not have a clear picture to communicate or is writing deliberate mush. Either way, the reader deserves to be angry.

Don't write: "He felt as if he might become ill. Gradually, he came to believe he could not quell the sickness rising from his abdomen. He thought the feeling of being nauseated would overcome him," when you mean: "He threw up."

Avoid splitting hairs in images and emotions. Check your Incident to be sure you haven't written either half-emotions or fuzzy images. Every time you read a form of the words *think, perceive, conceive, seem, believe,* or *feel,* an alarm should go off in your writer's brain alerting you to rewrite the imprecise language.

Just as bad is overwriting, or re-creating minute details of a setting. Establish a clear dominant impression and get on with the story. If you need further details, add them as you go. Don't drag out every burp, grunt, and wheeze as a character grows angry.

Once you clarify images and emotions, be consistent with the stand you've taken. Never change on whimsy or by coincidence. Once established, only the characters influenced by their realistic, competing motivations—and not the author—can reorder images and emotions.

One modern-day best-selling author writes characters that spew filth at each other in one Incident, then fall into bed in the next. I don't object either to spew or to bedrooms, but nothing happens between Incidents that would justify a change of heart, making such behavior laughable (all the way to the bank, I suppose).

Last of all, check for intentional imprecision you've used as a way to artificially create mystery or build suspense. To borrow from Robert Fulghum: *Play fair.*

Don't withhold details crucial to understanding the story just so you can spring a surprise later.

When you leave out necessary detail, that's cheating. A very successful best-selling author wrote a novel in which law enforcement principals discuss a crime at the front of the story. At the tale's end, the heroic character solves the crime with a deduction that arises directly from information given during the conference, information so basic that only a moron would not have suspected the surprise murderer from the start. This was not an insignificant detail planted and overlooked by the reader, either. If you read the book, the instant you saw the solution in print, you thumbed back to the front and asked why the heroic character didn't find the killer in the first chapter. Answer: Because the author needed to fill the space between the planted detail and the story's climax with a novel. The author cheated.

GIVE MOUTH-TO-MOUTH TO DROWNING VERBS. Official writing teaches us the drowning verb syndrome. Here's an example that demonstrates: "The secret committee held a meeting to give consideration to Ambrose's plan. Committee members made the decision to give their approval to it." As opposed to "The secret committee approved Ambrose's plan." It's safe to assume the members met before bestowing their approval.

Unlike the global searches, these aren't so easy to catch. The trick is to look for the verb form that's being drowned in weak verbs, such as *give, hold, make, involve,* and *is.*

TEST FOR SINGULARITY. Don't ramble. Wordiness diffuses ideas. Don't juggle too many story lines at one time. Keep the reader on track throughout the story. If you get tricky and zig when he zags, you could lose him. Fact is, you could get lost yourself.

One idea for each sentence; a single topic for each paragraph; a singular plot point for each Incident. And stick to the main story line in writing your novel's first draft.

This rule isn't as hidebound as it seems. I wouldn't dream of outlawing big words, complicated sentences, and richly textured Incidents in complex stories. All I'm saying is, even intricate sentences, paragraphs, and Incidents ought to keep to one point. And, of course, every Incident should somehow lead to the climactic Incident and the novel's logical ending. Is it too much to ask you to let the reader know where you're going?

The fixes for lapses in singularity? Simple.

- Break violating sentences into shorter sentences, each with a single idea, no matter how many words you use.

- Separate rambling paragraphs into multiple paragraphs, each with a single topic.

- Create two Incidents if any one Incident is causing too many problems.

- Work on subplots only after you've finished the main story line.

RUN THAT REI SCAN FROM TIME TO TIME. This time you're not as worried about meeting the goals we set earlier. You're looking for problems you may have written back into the story in your revision. As you mellow out part of the Incident, have you turned every dialogue exchange into the passive voice? That's neither good nor bad unless you think it's so. The REI lets you take the vital signs of your writing as you move along. If you've deliberately slowed the pace of your story below the REI standards, who can argue with you? Certainly not me.

It's always a good idea to run an occasional word count on the manuscript in any case. If you stay tuned to your novel's length, you'll be sure to avoid overwriting—remember 70,000 to 80,000 words is about right for most fiction categories. If it looks like you'll be short on word count, pump up the conflict in important Incidents rather than padding out narration. If you're long, at least you know you've finished the main story line. You can keep the rest of the novel lean without damaging the story.

READ YOUR MATERIAL ALOUD. Read into a tape recorder. As you play back your Incidents, listen for the following:

- Excessive musings. When a character starts brainstorming with herself, weighing options and grappling with decisions, she's musing. This isn't objectionable in brief passages, but ask yourself whether such an internal monologue might better be put into action, dialogue, or the trash bin.

- Droning explanations. If you hear an explanation that sounds like a classroom lecture, recast the passage.

- Tongue twisters. Fix 'em.

- Repetitions. Cut.

- Faulty rhythm. If the material sounds choppy when you read it, although there's no coinciding action, smooth out the passage. If it drones on, you'll hear it.

- Narcoleptic passages. If the passage's content bores even you, start rewriting. Juice it up or cut it out.

- Narrative blunders. If you commit sins against the fictional truth you've established, you'll hear them on tape.

- Strained emphasis. If you hear yourself putting on too much of a radio voice to make a passage understood, you'll know the words on the page can't carry the freight alone. You have work to do.

GET SOMEBODY TO READ THE MANUSCRIPT TO YOU. If you can, it's going to have to be somebody who loves you. Or somebody you hire, I suppose. Some programs have a voice feature that will read text to you. I've tried these, and, heck, I'll be frank about it: I hate them.

When you're finished revising this draft, your writing ought to sing. (Or maybe you can get somebody to sing your novel back to you.) In any case, let's see if we can tune your story to the highest level in the next steps of revision. Beginning with ...

WRITING IN THE WHITE SPACE

If you have studied painting, sculpture, photography, or graphic design, you're already familiar with the concept of white space, that is, negative space, as a means to improving the composition of an image.

The technique I admire most in the true artists among our writers is the ability to communicate a point seemingly without writing about it. Or, as I call it, writing in the white space.

Mirroring

A common example of writing in the white space is the description written as a reflection. Rather than write the obvious outright narrative description, as in ...

> He was tall, six-feet-two, with a nose to match, tall, thin, and straight.

That's the author talking. Contrast that with: He caught sight of his six-feet-two reflection in the window of a bagel shop, paused, and studied his thin, straight nose both in profile and straight on. Straight on, he decided, always show his nose to her straight on. Never from the side.

Same information, different approach. One that gives the facts without stopping the story as if to say, *I'm going to describe somebody now.* At the small cost of a word increase, we see the reflection through the character's eyes, not the author's keyboard. We see action, both actual and implied—it is suggested that the character turns his head from side to side to study his own profile. Plus we learn something about the character's personality. He's vain about the nose.

That's writing in the white space.

Other techniques of writing in the white space follow.

The Smash Cut

The term *smash cut* comes from film writers. It implies a jarring, abrupt Incident change. For instance, the closing shot in one Incident might be a beautiful woman sipping her Folgers as the red sun rises over the mountains. Smash cut to the red fireball of an ear-splitting terrorist explosion over the mountainous landscape of a city skyline.

The fiction writer's smash cut can save a lot of miles in writing transition (and/or explanations of how a character got from one place to the other). The best way to illustrate this is by example.

A chapter's ending sentence:

> He was so proud of himself and couldn't wait to hear what Mama would say when he told her what he had done.

Followed by a page break and the opening of a new chapter:

> "You imbecile," Mama said. "You scant-wit, slack-jawed, mouth-breathing, knuckle-dragging idiot."

Nothing but the turn of a page stands between the character's wondering what Mama will say and what Mama actually says. No taxi ride. No bus transfer. No subway graffiti. Not even a description of how a proud son broke the news to his incredulous mother. The writer assumed that you could assume anything you wanted between his wondering and her reacting. The result's better, too.

Dialogue That Eliminates the Need for Narration

One more thing I'd like to point out is dialogue's ability to help you write in the white space. Take a look at Mama's line of dialogue above. The word choice indicates enough emotion. No need to say, *Mama said in disbelief*, or *Mama said angrily.*

Letting the Character Tell

The conventional wisdom holds that you should always show, don't tell. Not always. Here's an example where telling works because the characters are doing the telling …

> "What?"
>> "What do you mean, what?"
>> "I mean why you wearing that stupid smile?"

No author to tell you that the first character is smiling; no narrator to say that it's a stupid smile. Both drop out of sight so the character can tell you that the smile exists and that he considers it stupid.

Showing by Consequence Rather Than Action

Sometimes you can achieve a powerful effect by skipping over the action and showing the result.

> "I told you not to talk to me like that, Randy," she said. "I told you what I was going to do if you talked to me like that again."
>> He blew a stream of air between his lower lip and upper teeth. The sound reminded him. "Get me a brew."
>> "What did you say?"
>> "You deaf? I said get off your butt and get me—"
>> He cradled his nose in his hands, huffing blood through his fingers and down his elbows.
>> "See?" she said, standing over him, her fist still balled. "See what you made me do?"
>
> No windup, no punch, just the punch's effect.

The Narrator Talks to the Character, Not the Reader

Did you notice in the previous characters' dialogue exchange that the narrator resisted the temptation to say the sound he made with his lip and teeth reminded him of a beer can snapping open? That would be telling the reader. Instead, the character said, "Get me a brew." Some readers would get the notion that the sound of blowing between upper teeth and lower lip can sound like a beer opening. If not, they didn't miss anything important.

Do, Don't Tell.

Once in a while, if you keep your eyes open, you'll find an opportunity to exploit an interactive narrative device.

> One-thousand-one, one-thousand-two, one-thousand-three.
> *He clenched his eyes and plugged his ears. Any second now. She should see the snake.*
> One-thousand-four.
> *She should be screaming by now.*

Rather than tell that the character counted to three, the narrator does the counting. Thus, the reader counts along with the character.

CREATE TIE BACKS AND TRANSITIONS

Tie backs and transitions are two ways of layering your story with depth and texture. First, transitions. When you're writing, how do you keep the story in motion from one paragraph to the next, from Incident to Incident, and from chapter 12 to chapter 13? Any number of ways. Let's look at some.

USE OBVIOUS TRANSITIONAL WORDS AND PHRASES. *Later, an hour later, next morning, when summer came, soon after.* Like that. Don't avoid this technique just because it's simple. One caution: Don't get so hung up on moving the reader along that you have to hold his hand. You can overuse this device. Beware.

REFLECT WORDS AND PHRASES. Words in a previous segment are repeated outright in the opening of a new segment. You end a chapter with "No way around it—she'd have to compel him to talk." You open the next chapter with, "She blocked his path and said, 'We have to talk.' "

REFLECT CONCEPTS AND IDEAS. Using the previous example, you open the next chapter with:

> She followed him into the Ritz-Carlton, then into the men's room. He saw her in the mirror, his eyes showing all the whites. Before he could open his mouth, she

shoved his face into the wall. "Start singing, creep, before I feed you the big pink mints out of the urinal."

JUST DON'T. The best way of all to get from one place to the next is just to go there and begin writing. Readers are clever enough to follow a well-written, logical story line, even one with flashbacks and detours. One of the most dreadful habits a beginning writer can develop is wasting time and words moving characters around.

Take that last example, the woman vowing to confront the man. No next day, no cab ride from O'Hare International Airport, no tip for the doorman, no questions of the concierge, no debating with herself about how to approach her mark. She follows the guy into the bathroom, overpowers him, and threatens him. Forgive me the immodesty, but I like it.

How to Tie Back

Transitions in reverse are tie backs. For your novel to transcend a feeling of "this happened, then this happened, then that," you must establish relationships between the action of one Incident and any number of previous Incidents. Here are several devices you can use.

- **Cause and effect.** Easy, if you've followed all the logic to get here. You establish that a character wants something (a worthy goal) and acts to get it. Why? Motivation, of course. This causes a ripple effect. In later Incidents a worthy adversary produces obstacles, creating problems. Never write so subtly that the reader can't pick up these fundamental relationships, even in a mystery.

- **Logical progressions.** Your heroine will die unless she finds the antidote for the poison in her system. As the novel proceeds, so must the degree of her illness.

- **Foreshadowing and planting.** Remember the film *Jurassic Park*, when the paleontologist Alan Grant talked about raptors hunting in packs and later they saw it happen before their eyes during the climactic Incidents? And remember the opening image of the fossil claw? Did you catch its reflection later in the movie when the raptor tapped its claw while hunting the grandkids in the kitchen?

Let's see what you can do. Using all the techniques described in this chapter, get on with writing your first, most favorite master Incident. When you're finished, don't start on your second Incident. Revise the draft of that first Incident according to principles of the next chapter.

ADDING TEXTURE TO YOUR NOVEL

TEXTURIZE WITH SUBPLOTS. When you introduce a subplot, give it a different color font and a separate string of colored Incident checklists. In *Slumdog Millionaire*, Jamal's brother, Salim, got involved with the mob. That's a subplot. It has its own story line with one very dramatic Opener in the film and another, even more dramatic Closer with several Incidents in between.

Several considerations for subplots:

Subject your subplots to the same rules of rising action and tension that you subject your central story line and individual Incidents to. Subplots should not remain static but should always move toward triumph over tragedy. If you can write subplots as "a novella within a novel," the entire story benefits.

Always keep subplots tied to the main story line, even if those ties are not visible to all the characters. Stories with several subplots that keep their connections to the main story line always seem to me to be more interesting.

If you can, write subplot story lines straight through, from beginning to end. In a novel that has several subplots, I find it harder to write several Incidents of the main story line and then to plug in one subplot Incident, then another from a different subplot. Far easier to write the main story line from front to end and then to write each subplot in the same manner. You can make revision tracker notes to yourself as you go. Doing so will help keep up momentum. Then, when you have finished each at least in rough draft, you can plug Incidents into the proper place within the main story line.

Resolve important subplot issues at or near the climax of the central story line. If you can work out a number of issues at crunch time in your story, the reader will be enthralled. This doesn't mean your subplots must last through an entire story. In figure 7 Subplot 2 might involve a meeting between the heroic character and a love interest who is killed by the villain in the Point-of-No-Return Incident. **Caution:** Don't throw so many issues into the resolution of the climax that it clutters the story. Better to simplify than to dilute the effect of your resolution.

TEXTURIZE USING THAT SEEMINGLY TRIVIAL DETAIL, THE TIE BACK. Write a small object or event into the narrative, early in the story. Left in plain sight, characters and readers overlook it until it comes into play at some critical moment late in the story. This technique works when the detail isn't *too* obvious. Remember in vintage films how the director would subject such a detail to an extreme close-up? And just in case we didn't get the possibility that it would later come to play an important part in the story, the soundtrack hit you with a crescendo of ominous music. Nowadays you need to hire a crew of investigators to pick up such minor details.

But the best trivial details work when you have planted them well enough so that when they crop up, readers recognize them instantly and even give themselves a slap on the forehead for overlooking them earlier. Think about it: *If you can get readers slapping themselves, you really do have participation, don't you*?

Usually, in writing a first draft, you don't have a handle on all the details, trivial or otherwise. That's what makes it so convenient to texturize with tie backs. How you do it? Simply go straight to the climactic or other important Incidents of your story, usually toward the end of the book. Find a detail that's critical. Then look back in the book to see if you can locate an earlier spot to plant that detail in plain sight.

TEXTURIZE WITH SEEMINGLY SMALL WORDS AND IDEAS. I like this technique best of all the texturizing devices, because you can enrich the manuscript by using them in a number of variations. Here are two:

> **Repeat a distinctive thought or phrase of dialogue** in the story. This connects an earlier part of the story to a later one without having to rely on an overt transitional device. Television shows frequently overuse this technique, giving one character a pet phrase that he repeats ad nauseum. One way to vary the device is to give it a different meaning each time it's used. On *Seinfeld*, all the principal characters would use the same phrase, often with different meaning, all in the same Incident, creating a device all of its own.

> **Plant the story's ending in the first thousand words.** Simply review your ending. Transplant a telling word or thought directly into the beginning of the story. Massage the context so it doesn't become a crude giveaway, but rather a well-crafted throwaway line that turns out to being not so throwaway after all. Between the beginning and the end, don't fall victim to the temptation to continue hammering away on that singular thought or phrase. Let it lie. Clever readers will pick up on it.

TEXTURIZE USING CONSISTENCY OF CHARACTER. Both motivation and cause and effect come into play during texturizing. Review each character's goals and motivations. Then take a look at every situation where the character comes into play. Satisfy yourself and your readership that the character's behavior is consistent with her motivation and that consistently motivated behavior causes predictable effects. Look at small situations as early as you examine the big events. Look for opportunities to reaffirm character consistency in the smallest ways.

Finally look for changes as characters develop, either growing or deteriorating. Characters often do change. Your job as writer demands that any change is consistent with sufficient motivation and not just the whim of the author. Then, once that change is established, decide whether the character remains consistent to the end of the story. Or whether she backslides. Both are elements of effective texturizing.

TEXTURIZE USING CONFLICTING POINTS OF VIEW. When you tie back characters who are in conflict to an event that involved both of them, look for opportunities to show how they differ in their recollections. When a significant event occurs within the novel, don't let your characters forget it happened.

TEXTURIZE USING THAT ELEMENT OF SURPRISE. Nothing texturizes like surprise. As you revise your fiction, take a close look at Incidents that might be too methodical, too predictable. It's one thing for you to remain true to plausible motivation and believable cause and effect, and quite another for your story to plod forward, technically correct but boring.

I'm not talking about trick endings where you unmask the narrator as the heroic character's pet kitten. That's too stupid for words. And I don't mean you should pull the rug out from under your readers at the climactic Incident or other major moments.

Rather, I suggest you use one of the strategies we discussed in chapter 1 to find an unexpected ending to an Incident, an unpredictable sentence to finish off a paragraph, or an unusual word choice to color a sentence. Surprise your readers. Better yet, surprise your characters. Best of all, when you can, surprise yourself.

If you use this checklist faithfully as a way of looking at your writing, you will find ways to improve it and move it down the path toward the big book. No matter what, in the end you'll have improved the quality of your work.

> *Creating the experience that sells your story.*
>
> Here's what you're going to do in chapter 9:
>
> - Get real about what might happen when you submit your novel.
> - Identify the selling points of your story.
> - Analyze the marketplace.
> - Prepare your pitch.
> - Prepare your package.

SELL BY PARTICIPATIONS?"

Remember what I told you a few pages ago? *It ain't art—it's bidness.* Now more than ever, forget all you ever learned in your lit classes about musical language, symbolism, and theme. Put aside any ideas I may have planted about characterization, pace, and rhythm. From now on, it's selling—naked commerce—not far from peddling fruit and vegetables from your garden. The produce has to be good, and it must be presented well. If your peaches look wonderful but taste bland and woody, it's no sale. If the tomatoes are blemished and stinky, nobody cares that you grew them organically in soil from the Nile Delta and fertilized them with the ground bones of the pharaohs.

Sell your novel not with the idea that publishers should give you and your agent money for it, but with the notion that buying your manuscript will make money for them. It's the concept of participation. An editor or agent is asking,

Why should I care about this novel more than any other of the eighty-nine I have to deal with this week?

You won't find many guarantees in publishing, but here's one you can take to the bank: If an agent believes she can make money selling your novel to a publisher, she'll handle it. If a publisher believes he can make money selling your novel to the public, he'll buy it. Period.

Once you get it into your skull that you must sell your product to every level of the industry, you've taken a huge first step.

Oh, and this might be a good place to point out that you're not finished polishing your manuscript. That comes later in chapter 10.

I suggest you send your pitch before polishing. That way, the pitch can be out there working for you and you can feel a renewed sense of urgency to do the work in chapter 10.

Start by understanding the people within a literary agency or a publishing house that you must sell to. People at every level can reject you. Here's a typical journey for material you submit.

- **Mail handler.** This person opens and sorts mail and directs it up the food chain. Even she might have rejection power. If the agency or house has a rule of accepting query letters only, she'll send back a full manuscript. You wasted all that postage and nobody ever read a word of your novel. To impress this person, you need do only two things: 1) follow every rule on how to submit to the letter; 2) make her believe that it's a mistake to reject you by creating a single tiny spark of fear.

- **First reader.** This is usually an entry-level employee, intern, or outside person hired to screen out the chaff. Fully 80 to 90 percent of material will be rejected at this level. If you've already made the cut by following the rules for submitting, make this woman believe that you can help her climb the career ladder by choosing your book as her first hit novel.

- **Associate.** An assistant or secretary will sometimes screen material for an editor or agent. The associate will likely have veto power on anything sent up by a first reader—which means the associate can reject you. He might also add remarks, highlight intriguing queries, and push your novel to his boss. He might have authority to request sample chapters or a full manuscript. Help this poor guy get through the day—he's read so much sleep-inducing material already, and he really wants to move up in the world. Let your novel be the story that energizes his career.

- **Editor or agent.** She'll skim your material and either reject it or ask for more. Will she buy your book if she likes it? Not right away. The selling job goes on. She will probably ask a colleague to read the material. If both agree on the material's potential, they'll present a package to a company acquisitions meeting. Whether in a publishing house or an agency, your manuscript will be evaluated for its sales potential, marketing strategy, budget, and other business considerations, including the amount of money you might receive for your work. You win over this person by giving her a truckload of arguments she can use to make a pitch to the final decision makers.

You won't attend the acquisitions meeting, so why am I telling you about it? To remind you of the nature of this process: business, selling, money. No matter how well it is written, your manuscript will be rejected unless an agency or publishing house can muster a reasonable expectation of making money on it. As they say in the Mafia movies: "Nuttin' personal; just business."

You may never discover why you get rejected at any stage of the process. Possibilities include lack of time, lack of focus, lack of talent, lack of a self-addressed stamped envelope (SASE), or lack of a market. Others: The book is not right for the house or agency, or the list of books or authors in a category is full. Sometimes there is no reason; it's just bad luck.

How can you overcome such a wall of obstacles? Three great ways: good writing and a great story; using every element of the principle of participation; refusing to waste other people's time.

Nothing but cash flow is more valuable than time in the publishing business—a high-energy industry filled with deadlines and juggling of projects. Every contact you make should indicate you're not going to waste anybody's time. That's what's behind the five steps that follow.

STEP 1: IDENTIFY A DOZEN DEALERS FOR YOUR PRODUCT

Pick six. Either six agents or six publishing houses. Check the current annual directories like *Novel & Short Story Writer's Market* and *Guide to Literary Agents*. Read every entry. Identify all the people who either publish or represent material similar to what you've written. Narrow your list to your top choices. Then carefully recheck the directory entries so you know exactly what the guidelines of each agency or house are in regards to method for contacting, SASE, and the like.

Should you market to six agents first or send your materials to publishers first? Not to be wishy-washy, but I feel strongly both ways. I collected more than fifty rejections from editors for my first novel, some of them encouraging. Once I had the offer of a contract from an editor, he told me to go agent shopping. I did and was able to obtain my first agent over the phone. Once you find an agent to represent you, the job of selling belongs to him, and you can continue writing.

Later, during a time when I had no agent, I marketed to agents and had some great results. Either way will work. If you want to research this in greater depth, there are some helpful books that feature advice from agents. Get Jeff Herman's *Guide to Book Publishers, Editors, & Literary Agents* or any other guide that quotes the professionals. You probably have a gut feeling on the subject anyhow and you're going to take the advice you want to hear.

Believe me, I know the feeling. That doesn't help you very much, but here's something that will: When you search any of the literary guides, you're likely to find information on what agents love and hate about the material that they read. You should pay attention to these specifics. Why risk getting a standard rejection form for your wonderful piece of work when the only reason it wasn't read was because the agency refuses to open attachments to e-mails and that's the way you sent it? If you had read their rules for submission, you would have pitched your novel in 250 words inside the body of your contact e-mail the way they asked you to.

My advice? Market your work to six agents first. After the last of those sales letters has gone out, market to six publishing houses.

If you do it the other way, no harm will come to you. No matter how you do it, you're going to go through the same drill.

STEP 2: IDENTIFY THREE DISTINCTIVE ASPECTS OF YOUR NOVEL

As always, think business. How is your novel different from what's already in the marketplace, yet not too different?

Sell your novel as fresh, distinctive, and radically new, but not radical, and always in line with the kinds of books they've been selling or representing.

As a rule, you won't find the publishing industry overpopulated by mavericks and gamblers. Whereas lots of editors have lost their jobs for buying stinkers, nobody ever got fired for rejecting a manuscript from an unknown.

Strip away the glamorous aura they generate about themselves and giant publishing houses look like garden-variety plastic manufacturers—with executive trolls trying to climb their career fire poles and the grunts just trying to eke out a living. Try to persuade, not overpower, always adhering to the logic that fresh material will improve the publisher's lot in life.

Identify your novel's distinguishing elements. If it's a Western, maybe you took an original approach of realism rather than romanticizing the Old West. If you were able to add authenticity because you spent last fall rounding up cattle in Montana, by all means mention it.

Suppose you wrote a romance about high-school sweethearts whose twenty-year marriage had to end in divorce before they could fall in love at the adult level? That might be a fresh twist.

If you're an expert in a field you've woven into your novel's fabric, you'll want to identify that as a distinctive aspect.

Is your novel based on a historical event? A new science? A new take on an old science? An unsolved crime? That's distinctive.

If you know of a growing market trend or regional news event that hasn't gone national, tell somebody.

If any aspect of your novel is likely to make money for the publisher or agent, by all means, identify it in your first contact.

Above all, remember that agents and editors will care about your career only if they believe that your success will build their own. Any package you send should pass muster of the PARTICIPATIONS?" checklist.

Pitching With PARTICIPATIONS?"

Let's say you have a sparkling manuscript, every page a model of our checklist on every point. If you get somebody to read it, your novel will sell itself.

But those elements can also perform a sales job for you.

Let's look at how those points that can help you.

Precision. Be precise in your words and ideas in every area of the pitch. Don't let even your bio sound as if it comes from one of those boilerplate résumé books.

Action. Use the active voice. And now that you've gotten into the habit of writing active verbs and concrete nouns, don't stop doing it in the pitch.

Relevance. Why should readers care about your book? If you can make the case that lots of readers, indeed, millions of readers care about the issues you're tackling in your novel, editors and agents, being smart people will make the connection. I wrote a crime novel once when I was between agents. As I was working at the pitch, I read of a horrific crime on the front page of *The New York Times*. I literally yanked the headline and story from the news, dropped it into a query letter, and faxed it to fifty agencies. More than twenty-one agencies responded to my fax attack in one positive way or other, several within hours.

Tales. Turn your pitch into a coherent story. And within that story with its beginning, middle, and end, add a dozen tiny tales. The tales come from the novel. Use illustrations from life. Go to YouTube to see if you can use one of the fabulous stories going viral this week.

Imagery. Create images in your pitch. Don't overwrite, but do make your letter come to life with verbal pictures.

Conflict. Refer to the distinctive conflict within the story, a version of conflict editors and agents might not have seen before.

Irony. Don't take yourself too seriously. Editors and agents read so much material that you can make a good impression if you can just make them smile. I know. I'm an editor. I fall for it every day.

Pacing. Don't let your material drag. Give your letter a beginning, a middle, and an ending. Measure each segment using the REI scale. Revise to set the pace appropriate to each segment. Do the same for the synopsis.

Aspirations. Refer to the many ways readers would be better people by reading your material.

Tone or voice. That's self-evident, isn't it? Sound confident, not cocky. Be businesslike, not pedantic. Be enthusiastic, not giddy. Try to infect editors and agents with your own feeling for the novel and mastery of tone and voice, even in a pitch.

Ideal. The REI. Rid your material of the passive voice. Clamp that REI to your text like a dog bite and rag it around until it meets every writing goal. An agent might reject it, but she would have a good read.

Only two thousand words. Be brief. In publishing, time is money. A one-page letter, a one-page synopsis.

Novelty. Everything about your story should set it apart from any other submission that agent had read in the last month.

Surprise. Your language. Your approach. Your novel. Your characters. Find a way, without being cute or tricky, to pull a couple of surprises.

Questions. At a minimum, ask: *May I send sample chapters?*

Quotes. If you can't get a blurb from another writer or editor, find a way to use a slice of dialogue, your best excerpt from the story. At a minimum, your tone should engage agents and editors to the point where pin your pitch to the office bulletin board.

Write a Targeted Killer Sales Letter

Two considerations apply to targeting. First, address your sales letter to a specific person. Phone the agency or publishing house and ask whether the agent or editor listed in the directory still works there. If so, ask if she has a new job title. If not, ask for the name of whomever is accepting submissions. The idea is to avoid mailing in the blind to "Whom It May Concern," "The Editor," or "Mr. Agent Man."

Second, review each directory entry to be sure you're sending precisely the package the company wishes to see. If the agency wants a one-page cover letter and the first twenty-five pages, send that (and not twenty-five pages from the middle of the book, either). If they want a letter and synopsis only, don't send a writing sample—the first impression you make will be either that you can't follow instructions or that you won't. Neither is good.

The Three-Part Sales Letter

PART ONE: Open with a version of your Nugget Statement. Rewrite it in letter form:

> Please consider (publishing/representing) my romance novel, *Heart of Lead*. My story is about (write in your Nugget Statement).

This tells the agent or editor what you're selling without wasting time on introductions. If you've written a snappy nugget, it will act as a sample of your writing ability. Now is not the time to stretch your summary to one hundred words.

Now I've suggested a safe opening. I hesitate to tell you to do as I do, but I never play it safe. Earlier I told you about my fax attack. I still remember the essence of my opening line to that fax pitch:

> This is one of those rare moments when a novel is ready for America at the very moment the topic is all over the front page of *The New York Times*.

I could prove my claim. I referred to the story in the *Times* and told how it applied to my novel. I revealed the nugget info. I made a huge point of saying I had finished the novel. I listed my writing credits. Above all, I kept it brief. To uncoil six feet of fax paper on the agent's floor would have been suicidal.

If you could open with a provocative, true statement like that, you should. Then get to the nugget.

PART TWO: Tell why your novel is in a class by itself and likely to make money for the agency or publishing house. Be artful about it. Don't say something like "My novel is going to make us all rich." Rather, point out what's new, what's fresh, what's different. Tell who will read the novel, an audience that the publisher might not have considered. If you've thought of a business consideration that's not apparent in a reading of the nugget, bring it up.

PART THREE: Give the pertinent details. Essentials include a mention that the novel is completed, the word length, and relevant biographical information. That means if you've published articles or books, say so. If you're an expert in the field, bring it up.

Don't ramble. Keep this letter to one page. If the material is enticing, and your writing is coherent, the letter will do its job of selling. Extending your sales pitch to ten pages won't help.

Your last words should ask for the sale. The question part of PARTICIPATIONS?" Appeal for a decision: *May I send you a writing sample?* Or the first three chapters. Or the completed manuscript. Something that requires a response.

STEP 4: ENCLOSE A KILLER SYNOPSIS

Flesh out your Nugget Statement to one page, double-spaced. Introduce your adversaries and keep to the main plotline—you don't want to muddle your sales pitch with endless subplots. Tell about the most exciting scenes in the novel. Reveal the ending. Don't be coy, as in: "Want to see how it turns out?" All that does is antagonize.

Finally, enclose an SASE so the agent or editor can either send a note asking for more material or break your heart with a rejection slip. Use a business-size envelope. Don't enclose postage for returning writing samples. Instead, send out freshly printed material every time. The return postage that would have paid for your materials' return will pay for a clean printing, and you won't have to worry about dog-eared pages making a bad impression on a second submission.

STEP 5: DO SUBMIT BY E-MAIL IF AN AGENT OR EDITOR ALLOWS IT

They will tell you so in their listing in a current *Writer's Market* or on their website. As with any submission, follow their directions explicitly. If they ask for two hundred words and insist that you do not attach files, guess what happens if you break the rules? *Click.* Did you hear that? That was the sound of your e-mail going to the trash bin.

MECHANICAL PRELIMINARIES

Step 1: Adopt a Professional Format for Your Manuscript

Avoid boneheaded mistakes. Make your manuscript look as polished as possible by doing the following:

- Double-space lines of type—it's an industry standard. Never single-space, even on drafts. Forget about the economies of saving paper. The fact is that you can edit your work best when it's double-spaced.

- Establish professional margins. Use an inch and a quarter left and right and an inch at the top and bottom. On first pages of chapters, leave a third to a half page of white space.

- Number pages in either the upper- or lower-right corner of the page.

- Identify pages in the upper left with your last name and one or more words from the title, as in "Smith-You Can Write."

- Write only on one side of the page. Don't even make notes to yourself on the backs of pages. It's too easy to overlook them.

- Never use any form of binding for your manuscript. Leave it as a stack of loose pages.

- Use standard paper: 20 lb., white, letter-size (8 ½" × 11", 22cm × 28cm).

- Avoid tricky typefaces. Use Times New Roman, Courier, Bookman, New York, or a similar serif typeface. The letters of serif types have feet and ears, short lines that stem from the upper and lower ens of letters. Don't use sans serif faces such as Helvetica and Avant Garde—they're harder to read in book-length works. Also, don't write long passages in italics. I use italics for book titles, of course. I use them as asides, a way for the narrator to think something or say something to herself and to the reader, something that she doesn't want known to the hero of villain. If my novel was growing into long passages of asides, I might use a different font instead of italics, say a sans serif font because although it's not ideal it is easier to read than large blocks of italics. You don't want anything to get in the way of participation. If your publisher has a different style for setting type, you're not going to have much say about it anyhow.

Step 2: Spell-Check Your Pitch Package

Don't rely on the spell-checker alone. Read through your own work to check your spelling as well. If your software contains a grammar check, run that as well, even if it becomes tedious. You want your work to be professional.

STEP 3: Get on With Your Life

Waiting for a response is the worst aspect of this business. I've had editors take thirteen months to respond to a sales letter. Here are two worthwhile activities for passing time.

1. Start a log for your submissions. Keep track of dates sent, items you sent in a given package, rejections, names of editors and agents, publishing houses, postage, and so on.

2. Get busy polishing in chapter 10 and then start another novel. Nothing occupies the mind more productively. Should your pitch work, you'll need something to send (at least a writing sample) to the agent or editor. And, if you're really productive and can get a second project going, you'll be able to offer the news of a second book in progress. If you sell the second first, you'll be able to remarket a first, unsold novel. Anyway you cut it, keeping at your craft is the best way to keep your sanity. Not to mention …

Bottom line: *To improve your writing, write.* Professionals can't afford to let their talents atrophy: Pianists keep sharp with constant practice, dancers dance, ballplayers hit, golfers swing, and singers sing. Yet the last thing the would-be writer wants to do is write while waiting. She wants to hear that the first effort is worth starting a second.

Every professional writer worthy of name knows you can't make a dime in the business without planting your butt in a chair and writing. So do it.

Should you receive nothing but rejections, review your sales letter, especially the aspects of your novel you thought were so distinctive. Try to find other, more mercenary aspects to tout in your next round of letters. Send a second dozen sales letters, half to agents, half to editors.

Should a rejection be personalized, try to glean something of value from it. Heck, just because they're rejections doesn't mean they're bad. I once received a rejection that included these words:

... compelling ... well written ... really jumps with energy ... I encourage you to send it to places like Avon, Bantam, or Dell.

I photocopied the rejection and sent it with a sales letter to all three publishers. Dell bought the novel, my first. Later I used it to sell *Writer's Digest* a story titled "Turning Rejections Into Royalties," published in the October 1988 issue. I'm using it again as an anecdote in this book—a lot of mileage for one rejection letter.

Should you be asked to send more material, follow instructions to the letter. Double-check your package before you mail it. On the outside of the envelope, write in bold letters **Requested Material**. That will prevent those pesky mail handlers and first readers from rejecting you out of hand.

For the same reason, the first line of your cover letter on second contact should read, "Here's the material you asked to see." Won't that be a thrill to write?

LAST WORDS ON PARTICIPATIONS?"

As I told you, I have this Website: www.writefromparadise.com

You will find a lot of stuff there for writers, including digital forms and pdf forms to download and print or load up and use at once. And a place for you to add your thoughts about my system, including complaints or criticism.

I've included some tools and experimental material for writers of nonfiction and corporate writers in any field except the very technical aspects of technical writing. Although ... I would argue that even technical writing could benefit from parts of this system. Participation applies in all fields, wouldn't you say?

Finally, I should urge you to get busy applying these ideas to your work. Remold them. Toss out parts you don't like. Invent your own system. Whatever. But do write. Novels don't get done by thinking about them.

In fact, I have a couple novels to write and rewrite, too. Just like you. Just like you, I want to get to the next level. For now, let's get busy putting a final polish on our novels.

STEP 10: Polish Your Novel to Best-Seller Standards While Your Sales Package is Out There Pitching for You

Pacing your finished novel to the level of a highly paid professional.

Here's what you're going to do in chapter 10:

- Evaluate the pace of every Incident in your novel.
- Revise to adjust the pace within each Incident that needs it.
- Evaluate the pace of your novel as a whole and graph its intensity level from beginning to end.
- Revise as necessary to reset intensity and pace.

THE ULTIMATE PACING TOOL

When you go to reader reviews on Amazon, the one comment you find most often when a lot of readers like a book has to do with pace. Comments like:

> I couldn't put it down.
> > I stayed up all night reading.
> > A real page turner.
> > The story was over so fast.
> > What happened to the time? I missed my train stop.

Those readers are telling you that they love the fast pace in a story. Every good novelist has a gut feeling about how to pump up the action in high-energy Incidents. And, obviously, every best-selling writer has this instinct for building pace and intensity, then letting off on the gas, then racing to the finish of a novel.

You, like every reader knows and loves the feeling when a high-paced story sweeps him away like a flash flood.

Wouldn't you like to learn how to do that?

Be prepared to have some fun.

Let's get started.

Measure the Pace of Each of Your Novel's Incidents

We'll use this incident pacing tool to chart each Incident.

INCIDENT PACING TOOL

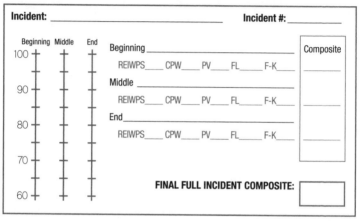

After setting the pace for Beginning, Middle, and End, run a final REI on the FULL Incident and subtract Flesch-Kincaid [F-K] score from the Flesch Readability score [FL] and enter the composite in the bold box above.

STEP 1. SELECT YOUR OPENING INCIDENT. Rule of thumb: If your novel is structured like Lee Child's *Gone Tomorrow*, you'll have short chapters of say, one thousand to fifteen hundred words. If you're writing a novel with longer chapters, that's no problem. No doubt each chapter is composed of any number of shorter Incidents. What you're looking for is an Incident that has a beginning, middle, and end and runs to no more than three thousand words.

Identify and number each Incident at the top. If your numbers correspond with your chapter numbers, you're in luck. If not (which is the more likely case), you have more than one Incident within each chapter so name and number each Incident. Just make note about what goes on in that Incident. You'll use these identifications later.

STEP 2. MARK THE BEGINNING, MIDDLE, AND END OF THE INCIDENT. If one segment has only fifty words or fewer, no problem. If you have an Incident that opens with a bang and closes with a whimper, no middle, no problem. Just measure what you have.

STEP 3. USING MICROSOFT WORD, RUN AN REI SCAN on each segment and record the results for each segment on the card:

STEP 4. SUBTRACT FLESCH-KINCAID FROM FLESCH READABILITY for each segmentand enter the result in the far right column. I'm sorry if this is beginning to sound like instructions for Schedule Z-3b of your 1040 long form, but we do have an aim here that will improve your writing, so bear with me. Besides, this is really simple.

STEP 5. USING THE THREE SCORES THAT YOU HAVE SO FAR, PLACE A DOT at the corresponding point on the vertical scale for the beginning, middle, and end of the Incident on the Incident Pacing Tool, as I've done on the next page. Then connect the dots. Now you can see the pace of your first draft.

STEP 6. EVALUATE. Hold this tool at arm's length and marvel. You can see at a glance whether this Incident varies in pace, either starting slowly, then speeding toward triumph or tragedy at a higher intensity at the end of the Incident, or whether it throttles down before picking up speed again. And of course, see whether the pace levels off, no matter what the intensity.

If your line forms a flat profile, as in our sample, even if your pace is high, the lack of variety will tire a reader and force you to press to keep it up so high. At a glance you know the pace of this segment in the novel needs variety.

Pick the spots where you'd like to slow the action and edit those parts of your Incidents. You might use the passive voice, longer sentences, and bigger words in an existing Incident. Or you might write a more leisurely Incident and insert it into the story. Or you might pick spots to elevate. With that in mind …

STEP 7. REVISE. If you expected this Incident to begin at a modest pace, then intensify upward all the way to the end of the Incident, these first numbers won't work for you. Clearly, you will want to dial up the pace in the middle segment of the Incident and really amp up toward the end.

Revise the scene and recheck segments with the REI scan until it looks and feels the way you want it to. At each revision, your numbers will tell their story and guide you in your progress.

It should be obvious that if you want to you could also revise the beginning segment to a lower REI standard, leave the middle segment alone, and

INCIDENT PACING TOOL

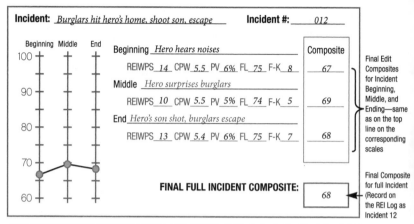

Incident: _Burglars hit hero's home, shoot son, escape_   **Incident #:** _012_

Beginning Middle End

Beginning _Hero hears noises_

REIWPS _14_ CPW _5.5_ PV _6%_ FL _75_ F-K _8_   Composite _67_

Middle _Hero surprises burglars_

REIWPS _10_ CPW _5.5_ PV _5%_ FL _74_ F-K _5_   _69_

End _Hero's son shot, burglars escape_

REIWPS _13_ CPW _5.4_ PV _6%_ FL _75_ F-K _7_   _68_

Final Edit Composites for Incident Beginning, Middle, and Ending—same as on the top line on the corresponding scales

FINAL FULL INCIDENT COMPOSITE: _68_

Final Composite for full Incident (Record on the REI Log as Incident 12

(After setting the pace for Beginning, Middle, and End, run a final REI on the FULL Incident and subtract Flesch-Kincaid [F-K] score from the Flesch Readability score [FL] and enter the composite in the box here. For example, in this example FL is 75 and F-K is 75, so the composite is 68.

dial up the ending segment just a bit. Only you can decide whether that will work for you. At this point in revising this Incident, you can stop worrying about the REI goals. Write your Incident the way you want it to read, and use this tool to achieve the intensity you want at each segment of the Incident. Suit your own taste and talent.

STEP 8. IF YOU'RE SATISFIED WITH HOW THIS INCIDENT READS, SELECT THE TEXT FOR THE ENTIRE INCIDENT and run one last REI scan on it in full. As you did before, subtract the number you get for Flesch-Kincaid from that of Flesch Readability. Enter your final full Incident result in the bold box. We'll use it later.

STEP 9. GO ON TO THE NEXT INCIDENT. Apply this tool again and again to each Incident, checking the intensity levels of each of the three segments of each Incident. Each time, after you have edited to your satisfaction, highlight all the text in that Incident and record the composite score as in Step 8.

Note for Corel WordPerfect users: To get the composite score for this tool, add the sentence complexity to the vocabulary complexity and subtract that result from one hundred to get a composite. Either composite will work on the Pacing Scale. That's because you're looking for variety as much as intensity here. And remember, participation-wise, variety can be a synonym for novelty.

COMPOSITE PACING SCALE—BASIC

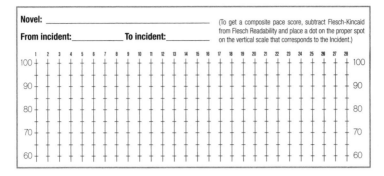

ADJUSTING THE OVERALL PACE OF YOUR NOVEL

Once you've evaluated every Incident, segment by segment, and recorded an overall Incident score, you're ready to evaluate the overall intensity or pace of your novel.

Nearly every writing workshop of any kind that I have seen shows the diagram of rising action, falling action, and overall climb to a maximum intensity at the climax of the drama, with the intensity killing off to the resolution and end of the story.

So far, nobody I know has specified how you can truly measure rising action, falling action, Incidents of maximum intensity, which should include the climax, and so on. Workshop leaders expect you to know how to do this, and you feel as if you have to fly by the seat of your pants.

No more. Now you have this simple tool.

A Novel's Overall Pace Evaluation Tool

You've already done the math to use this tool.

Just take that final composite number for each Incident, the one you recorded last after you finished revisions for each Incident.

One by one, plug the numbers into the vertical scale above by making a dot at the corresponding point on that scale for that Incident. You may need more than one sheet to get the job done. When you're finished, connect these dots (as shown on the next page) so you can see the intensity level rising and falling in your story.

Evaluate this result however you please. You know what you intended. As a rule, though, your major points of reversal in the story should be written to

COMPOSITE PACING SCALE—BASIC

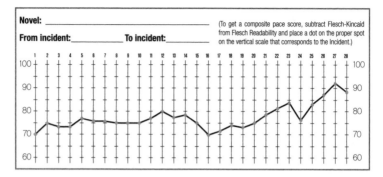

a high level of intensity, a fast pace. Your Opener should achieve a very fast pace. I would think the same for your PoNRI. And, of course, your climactic Incident within the Closer.

You know which of your Incidents you intended to be fast paced. If those critical Incidents lag, you know where you have to go to work.

Select the Incidents that you want readers to speed through and go to work on them. To make them stand out even more, you may want to have adjoining Incidents purposely lag.

No matter what you want, now you can see at a glance whether an Incident meets the goals you set for it.

The quickest way to pick up the pace is to cut long sentences down to size. Then cut long words from the piece and replace them with short ones. Use simple, declarative sentences, active voice, and short paragraphs. You know the drill from chapter 6.

Rule of thumb: You get the fastest pace in a high-energy Incident when the Incident averages ten words per sentence, a max of four characters per word in MS Word (one syllable per word in Corel WordPerfect), and 0 percent passive voice.

Set this higher Reading Ease Ideal for yourself when you have key Incidents that absolutely positively must read faster. Then edit the copy until you reach your goal.

SETTING THE ULTIMATE PACING STANDARDS

Once you have set a pace and a variety within Incidents (and across all the ins and outs of your novel), you may want to go back and juice up some Incidents to an even higher level.

COMPOSITE PACING SCALE—ULTIMATE

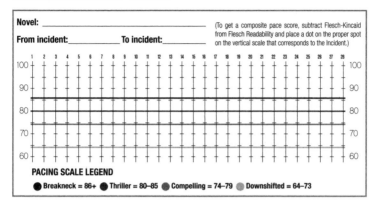

Novel: _____

From incident: _____ **To incident:** _____

(To get a composite pace score, subtract Flesch-Kincaid from Flesch Readability and place a dot on the proper spot on the vertical scale that corresponds to the Incident.)

PACING SCALE LEGEND

● Breakneck = 86+ ● Thriller = 80–85 ● Compelling = 74–79 ◐ Downshifted = 64–73

If that's the case, I've devised a set of standards you can use as a guide. Run an REI scan on an Incident or segment, using the chart above. Then review the descriptions of the various paces I've described below.

Simply edit to achieve the pace you want for a given segment or Incident. This can be a fun exercise. Just make sure you work on a copy of the original selection. If things get out of hand, you'll want to be able to get back to the original.

Pacing Standards

Breakneck Pace. To achieve a breakneck pace, revise to a composite REI of 86 or higher. When an Incident reaches this standard, your writing is at warp pace. My numbers come from the REI of Microsoft Word, by the way, because I write in Word but the same figure will translate in WordPerfect. If I'm writing a combat Incident or a major personal conflict, I want the writing to be in this zone.

Thriller Pace. A composite REI of 80 to 85. This is the pace of a thriller in a high-energy moment.

Compelling Pace. A composite REI of 74 to 79. This is the minimum range I'll accept in my writing. Except for an occasional dip above the downshift pace.

Downshifted Pace. A composite REI of 69 to 73. Once in a while, I'll let the action slow into this zone to give myself, my characters, and my readers a breather. But only for one Incident in a blue moon, so to speak.

Let me show you how this works.

Remember that fast-paced Lee Child excerpt I showed you on page 29? Here are the REI stats for that piece.

READABILITY STATISTICS	
Counts	
Words	**81**
Characters	365
Paragraphs	5
Sentences	13
Averages	
Sentences per Paragraph	2.6
Words per Sentence (WPS)	**6.2**
Characters per Word (CPW)	**4.3**
Readability	
Passive Sentences (PV)	**0%**
Flesch Reading Ease (FL)	**86.6**
Flesch-Kincaid Grade Level (F-K)	**2.7**
Composite REI (FL minus F-K)	**83.9**

Note the Composite REI of 83.9. That's what I call a *Thriller Pace*.

Watch what happens after I edit the piece lightly

> The square went quiet. A letter in a lit-up sign to my left sputtered on and off at random. I heard rats in the mulch behind me.
> I waited.
> Two minutes. Three.
> Thirty-nine minutes into my forty I sensed them far to my right. Footfalls, disturbed air, holes in the darkness. I saw figures in dim shadows.
> Seven men.
> Good news. The more now, the fewer later.

On the next page are the stats after revision, including an REI Composite of 88, which puts the segment into the Breakneck Pace category.

This is not to say I've improved the piece. Arguably, the action doesn't merit the machine-gun feel of the revision. I am merely showing how a piece of writing can read faster by edits in the final revision stages of your novel. If you have Incidents that need more cow bell, use this ultimate tool to measure your progress.

READABILITY STATISTICS	
Counts	
Words	**67**
Characters	289
Paragraphs	6
Sentences	12
Averages	
Sentences per Paragraph	2
Words per Sentence (WPS)	**5.6**
Characters per Word (CPW)	**4.1**
Readability	
Passive Sentences (PV)	**0%**
Flesch Reading Ease (FL)	**90.0**
Flesch-Kincaid Grade Level (F-K)	**2.0**
Composite REI (FL minus F-K)	**88**

On the next page is a sample of an ultimate revision of a novel.

The light gray line shows the pace before the final revision. I find it too flat for the first three-quarters of the story, don't you? I intend Incident 6 to be a high-energy bit of action, but it's anemic. So I rev it up during revision. I keep it going until the composite number meets or exceeds the Breakneck Pace standard.

You can see how I vary the pace in my final revisions by comparing the light gray line to the bold black line. Variety. Faster pace. Reaching for that feeling I want to give readers that they can't put down my story. Dragging readers in. Forcing them to play along. Participate.

You can have the ultimate control of your novel with this tool and the revision strategies I've shared here. You can do this. It can even be fun.

THE END

There you go. All the best tools and helpers I can put between two covers.

Use them, and know that they come with all the best luck I can wish you.

No more excuses. Because …

Bottom line: *The pacing tool, used with the REI as a guide to edit your fiction, will elevate your writing to the next level.*

COMPOSITE PACING SCALE—ULTIMATE

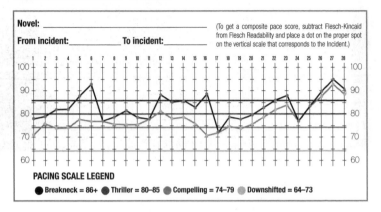

Novel: _____

From incident:_____ **To incident:**_____

(To get a composite pace score, subtract Flesch-Kincaid from Flesch Readability and place a dot on the proper spot on the vertical scale that corresponds to the Incident.)

PACING SCALE LEGEND

● Breakneck = 86+ ● Thriller = 80–85 ● Compelling = 74–79 ◌ Downshifted = 64–73

If you're a first-time novelist, these tools can cut years off the learning curve. If you've already published a novel and want to break out to the big book, these tools can get you to the tipping point and beyond. Use the tools and the elements of participation to sell agents, editors, sales staff, booksellers, and readers by the millions.

You can do this. You can write a novel. You can sell a novel. You can make it a best-seller.

Caution: The thing about selling a best-seller is you have to write it first.

So. Sit. Write. One Incident at a time. Then another. And another.

And so on. Good luck.

See you on the best-seller lists.

Index

ACIIDSS test, 66–69, 74–94
action, 11, 25, 36–39, 41, 64–69, 73, 76–77, 88, 150
adjectives, overuse of, 95–96
adverbs, overuse of, 95, 129
alliteration, 97
amateur mistakes, 94–98
Angle of Repose, 100
Apollo 13, 119
asides, 109
aspirations, 11, 29–30, 151
atomic flyswatters, 131
author's name, value of, 43
backstory, 57
Bernstein, Theodore M., 131
Big Chill, The, 37
Brown, Dan, 6–7, 10
cameo appearances, 32
Careful Writer, The, 131
characterization, 89
characters, 6, 44–59, 109
    antagonists, 36, 38–39, 41, 48–49, 72
    character arc, 52
    character kit, 48–49, 128
    consistency of, 144–145
    descriptions of, 44–46, 54–55
    digital filing system for, 49–59
    goals of, 36, 38, 41, 51, 57–59
    heroic, 35–40, 48, 53, 72, 123, 125.
    love interests, 48–49
    major, 49. *See also* characters, protagonists
    master, 48–49, 57
    minor, 49, 59
    motivations of, 20, 57–59
    names of, 46–48
    new, 124
    protagonists, 35–40, 48–49, 53–59.

voice of, 55–56. *See also* voice
Charles, Janet Skeslien, 24, 26, 28, 30, 33, 101
Child, Lee, 24–25, 29, 32, 85, 92, 98, 122, 158, 164
Clancy, Tom, 129
clichés, 96, 126, 130–131
cliffhangers, 32
climaxes, 73, 122, 143. *See also* Closers
Closers, 16–17, 37, 39, 41, 64, 69, 120–126. *See also* climaxes
coincidence, 123
conflict, 11, 27–28, 36–39, 57–58, 64–69, 73, 76, 80–82, 87, 123, 125, 151
conjunctions, 131
Cooper, James Fenimore, 17, 23
Cottage 13, 81–82
cover art, 43–44
Covey, Stephen R., 120
creativity, 106
Crichton, Michael, 97, 129
current events, as inspiration, 35
Da Vinci Code, The, 6, 10
Dearly Devoted Dexter, 39
Deerslayer, The, 17, 23
description. *See* imagery
Designing Women, 89
detours, 109
dialogue, 12, 32–33, 55–57, 64–69, 73, 76, 87–90, 140
Diehl, William, 61
divine intervention, 123
doublets, 133
dramatic tension, 58
Dunne, Dominick, 35
editing, 99–105, 108–109, 148

Elements of Style, The, 98
Ellen Foster, 100
ellipses, 131
e-mail submissions, 153–154
epic struggle, 37
Even Cowgirls Get the Blues, 54
experimental writing, 97–98
exposition, 123–124
fatal flaws, 37, 58
"Fenimore Cooper's Literary Offenses", 17, 23, 98
first impressions, 70
Flagg, Fannie, 100
flashbacks, 123
Flesch-Kinkaid scales, 104–105, 107–108, 160–166
Force Recon, 101
foreshadowing, 73
Frankl, Viktor, 87
Fried Green Tomatoes At The Whistle Stop Café, 100
Fulghum, Robert, 135
Gallo, Carmine, 31
genre, 40
Gibbons, Kaye, 100
gimmicks, 97, 125
Gladwell, Malcolm, 76
Gone Tomorrow, 24, 29, 91, 104, 122, 158
"Good Bad Books", 8
grabbers, 41, 43
grammar check, 103–104, 110, 128
Grisham, John, 99–100
Guide to Book Publishers, Editors & Literary Agents, 149
Guide to Literary Agents, 148
"Hanging Out At The Buena Vista", 100
headlines, 114–116
Help, The, 37, 44, 49, 56, 62, 70–71, 74, 98
Herman, Jeff, 149
hero/heroine. *See* characters, heroic; characters, protagonists
How Stella Got Her Groove Back, 100
How to Write Best Selling Fiction, 43
humor, 73, 76
Hunchback of Notre Dame, The, 54
ideas, 34–39, 41
imagery, 11, 27, 29, 64–69, 73, 76, 82–85, 151
Incidents, 15–21, 49, 63–66, 73–74, 76, 90–92, 110, 112–126, 128.
irony, 11, 28, 30, 33, 64–69, 73, 76, 85–87, 125, 151
Jaws, 43–44

Jobs, Steve, 31, 70
Jurassic Park, 142
Karon, Jan, 100
King, Stephen, 8, 18, 99–100
Koontz, Dean, 43–44, 76
language
  body, 130
  nonverbal, 88
  office, 96
Largent, R. Karl, 44
length, of novel, 19–20
Leonard, Elmore, 20, 54, 85–86, 98, 100
Lindsay, Jeff, 39
literary agencies, 147
literary agents, 148–149
Lonesome Dove, 38, 59, 91
Lost Symbol, The, 7
Lost World, The, 97
Lovell, James, 119
Lovely Bones, The, 86
Maass, Donald, 27, 57, 73
Man's Search For Meaning, 87
manuscripts, format for, 154
marketing, 146–156
McCarthy, Cormac, 8
McMillan, Terry, 99–102
McMurtry, Larry, 8, 38, 59, 91
mirroring, 138–139
Misery, 100
Moonlight in Odessa, 24, 26–28, 30, 33
New Song, A, 100
nouns, precise, 41
Novel & Short Story Writer's Market, 145
novelty, 12, 31–32
nugget statements, 40–42, 129, 152
Odyssey, The, 91
One True Thing, 100
Openers, 16–17, 64–67, 70–74, 99, 109–112, 126
Orwell, George, 8–9, 24, 69
Outliers, 76
overwriting, preventing, 19–20, 109, 135
pacing, 11–12, 28–29, 31, 89, 108, 115, 151
pacing tool, 157–165
paragraphs, short, 100–103, 105, 162
participation, 5–10, 12–13, 23, 41
PARTICIPATIONS?", 24–33, 98, 146–147, 150–151, 156
Perfect Storm, The, 49
Peters, Tom, 70

Pinker, Steven, 3, 13
plotline, 40–41
Point of No Return, 16, 73, 118–120, 143
point of view, 59–62, 67, 70, 145
"Politics and the English Language", 24
precision, 11, 24–25, 96, 150
Presentation Secrets of Steve Jobs, The, 31
Primal Fear, 61
publishing houses, 35, 147–149
punctuation, 89, 97, 110, 128–129
Q & A. See Slumdog Millionaire
questions, 12, 32, 151
Quindlen, Anna, 99–100
quotes, 151
reader reviews, 2, 4, 11–12
reading aloud, 137–138
Reading Ease Ideal, 1–2, 30–31, 105, 107–111, 131, 137, 151, 160, 163
reading level, 104–105, 107.
realism, 58
redemption, 125
relevance, 11, 25–26, 150–151
repetition, 97, 137, 144
research, 3–4, 12, 129
revision, 127–145, 159–166
rhythm, 89, 138
Robbins, Tom, 54
Rural Montana, 3
salability, 22–42
sales letter, 152
saving grace, 58
Schindler's List, 87
Screenwriting: The Art, Craft, and Business of Film and Television Writing, 39
Sebold, Alice, 8, 86
Seinfeld, 38, 144
sentences, short, 100–103, 105, 162
setting, 45, 73
Seven Habits of Highly Effective People, 120
Shakespeare, William, 106
Shakespeare in Love, 59
Shining, The, 18
Shutter Island, 44
singularity, test for, 136–137
Sixth Sense, The, 61
sketches, 17–19, 23, 35, 40–41, 75
Slumdog Millionaire, 10, 17, 32–37, 40–41, 44, 66–69, 86, 90–94, 116–119, 125
smash cut, 139

spell-check, 103–104, 128, 155
Star, 100
Steel, Danielle, 8, 99–100, 102
Stegner, Wallace, 8, 100
Stockett, Kathryn, 37, 44, 56, 70–71
stories. *See tales*
story line, 73, 88–89, 112–126.
Street Lawyer, The, 100
style, 75–77, 135–138
subplots, 124, 143
surprise, 12, 32, 64–69, 74, 76, 92–94, 124–125, 145, 151
suspense, 73
Swarup, Vikas, 34–35, 66
synonyms, 94–95, 130
synopsis, 153
tales, 11, 26–27, 64–69, 76, 90–92, 151.
10 Rules of Writing, 54, 98
texture, 141, 143–145
Thurber, James, 96
tie backs, 20, 141–144
title, working, 40, 43–44
tone, 12, 30, 70, 73, 126, 151
tongue twisters, 137
transitions, 20, 141–142
Twain, Mark, 16–17, 21, 23, 59, 91, 98
twist, 41
Tyler, Anne, 8
usage problems, 133–134
Updike, John, 39
verbs, 41, 84, 136
Verlaine, Paul, 108
voice, 151
   active, 77–78, 100–101, 105, 162
   changing, 126
   of characters, 55–56
   passive, avoiding, 110, 128
Walter, Richard, 39
word count, 109
words
   action, 78–80
   choice of, 55–56, 109
   eliminating, 129–134
   pet words, 131
   short, 100–101, 103–105, 131–132, 162
   weasel words, 96
writer's block, 18–19, 21
Writer's Digest, 8, 77, 156
Writer's Little Helper, The, 24
Writer's Market, 40, 153
Writing the Breakout Novel, 27, 57, 73